GREEK

First published in 2010 by
The Dedalus Press
13 Moyclare Road
Baldoyle
Dublin 13
Ireland

www.dedaluspress.com

ISBN 978 1 906614 17 1

Dedalus Press titles are represented in North America
by Syracuse University Press, Inc., 621 Skytop Road,
Suite 110, Syracuse, New York 13244, and in the UK by
Central Books, 99 Wallis Road, London E9 5LN

Cover image © Ela Kwasniewski / iStockphoto

The Dedalus Press receives financial assistance from
The Arts Council / An Chomhairle Ealaíon

GREEK

Theo Dorgan

DEDALUS PRESS
DUBLIN, IRELAND

ACKNOWLEDGEMENTS

Acknowledgements are due to the editors of the following in which a number of these poems, or versions of them, originally appeared: *The SHop, The Irish Times, Southword* and *Boulevard Magenta* (Irish Museum of Modern Art).

'Bread Dipped in Olive Oil and Salt' was published in *Best of Irish Poetry 2008* (Southword Editions, 2008), and in *The Sailor and the North Star* (Nobi Press, Tokyo, 2006), as were 'Inland', 'Over Delphi', and 'Honey Yoghurt' with translations by Nobuaki Tochigi.

'Running with the Immortals' was commissioned originally by Cork City Council, to mark the conferring of the Freedom of the City on the athlete Sonia O'Sullivan. The present version differs slightly from the version read on that occasion.

'Ithaca' was first published in *Answering Back*, ed. Carol Ann Duffy (Picador, 2007)

Earlier versions of 'Kato Zakros' and 'Taverna on the Beach' were published in *What This Earth Cost Us* (Dedalus Press, 2008)

'Orpheus' and 'Eurydice' were published in *From the Small Back Room*, a Festschrift for Ciaran Carson (Belfast, 2008)

An earlier version of 'Sappho's Daughter' was published in 1998 in a limited edition by Wavetrain Press, Dublin.

for Paula

Σύντροφο του Δρόμου

Contents

SAPPHO'S DAUGHTER

UNDYING

Begin, Begin Again

1

Flat hard light through the high window,
new shoes rapping on the polished parquet,
a drift of chalkdust hung on air.

My head still full of summer,
running and hurling, space.
A fresh year laid out before us.

Head of an argive in the new book,
helmeted, bearded, a temple above him,
a trireme below in the bay.

Fresh ink, fresh paper, the world
quietly opening to the south.
Where the swallows go.

Three hundred men and three men.
Sparta. The Isles of Greece.
Wave-tossed Odysseus. Alexander.

Ships and dark wine, sunlight under the pines,
grapes and sour olives, rough bright walls.
The childhood of the world.

Round tower on the copybook; last year's tales
of winter storms, of blood and plunder.

I turned my back to the north wind,
no interest in Vikings, in death for gold.
The South took all my heart.

That winter I learned we were poor,
climbing Fair Hill in the slanting rain
with leaking shoes, to hurl in the mud and cold;
I saw myself growing old there in a small world
and I refused. Some dream of otherwhere took hold.

2

And then, years of the life we must call real.
The Matter of Ireland, the long march
through work and love,
murder salting the bitter wind, our weary
earnest arguments, slow thought;
trying in small ways to do good; years
of dig where you stand and what
is my nation? Tedium and joy in equal measure,
the increments of age and rage slow burning;
work and escape, work and escape,
the pull between what claims you and what you choose.

The great, slant freedom of our craft:
we make it all up. The words choose me
and I accept them, straightbacked & stubborn:
Sounion. Shandon. Hermes. Athene. Home.

The nets we flee, and find; and what finds us.

Home is where the heart grows,
and she has all my heart whom I scarcely hoped to know,
her foot falls with mine in sweet accord
where the small boats nose at the quay
and lamb smokes on the spit at evening
as we puzzle the alphabet, familiar and strange,
the heat of the day softening our bones in the dusk.

3

The stepped lanes of Eressos are the lanes I dreamed
walking the stepped lanes of my native city.
The ships at twilight in the roads at Piraeus
are ships that sat heavy with night on Penrose Quay.
The pines at Fountainstown on the clay bluff
stand in the same deep solitude over Therma,
I am that boy still, in two places at once,
rapping his foot and soaring over rooftops.

I would lie down under the Hunter's moon,
the air heavy with pollen, the island a murmur,
and talk the day back to where we woke
in the cool of morning, the day fresh with resin.
Breakfast in the cafeneion, honey and yoghurt,
your eyes cool as the Aegean beneath, your hand
searching mine as we sit sideways to the sea.

Last night I dreamed us back in Kato Zakros,
walking the ruined palace in moonlight,
taxis revving at the last taverna, the waiters
chattering of Dublin to somebody sunburned.

The fish on Shandon glittered over the rimlit ridge,
there were hurlers shouldering and calling on the stone beach.

The postman woke us, you reached to brush my lips
and smiled: *Kali mera*, you said. *Kali mera* my one love.

4

We come and go.

To live your life is not so simple as to cross the sea.
The voice you turn from will sometimes find you out.

Making out from Aghios Kirikos, what, two days ago?
Wave-tossed and sober, an old song in my head.

Torann na dtonn le sleasaibh na long
ag tarraingt go teann 'n ár gceann fé sheol.

That schoolroom again, a long perspective opening back—
hills of West Cork, that deep indented coastline
and ships on the sea, from the south and west,
from the east; the blue inrush of history, outrush of trade.

Dousing sail this morning in the roads off Piraeus,
somebody old moving through me, coiling the lines.

Our friend from Therma walks with us in the agora,
something of my mother about her,
sizing it all up, caught in the whirl of talk,
her eyes glinting and shrewd, her hand a bird's beak
darting to palp fresh fruit, pluck coins from out her purse.
And something of my father in Stephanos at Agriolykos,
swimming out into the bay, still blue-eyed, hale at eighty.

You locked onto the tune in my head, murmured
Measaim gur súbhach don Mhumhain an fhuaim...
your fingers tightened in mine; something came clear:

What is my nation is not the same thing as what is my place.

Between one moment and the next, a breath of grace.
We found our stride, stepping from light into shade
and out into light again, buffeted by the traffic,
held in the sway of talk where Plato walked.
An ordinary day in Athens of Munster, soft-vowelled Attica,
schoolroom of polis and temple, birthplace of thought.

The white city of childhood that is everywhere the same.
This one life that is everywhere the deep-indented same.

Kato Zakros

It is called the Gorge of the Dead.
High overhead the burial caves
are punched into yellow rock.

Sand underfoot, and dust, everything clear, precise.
Your sandalled foot falls there, and there, and there—
mesmeric clarity of stone and asphodel,

the exact blue of the scarf that binds your hair.
You carry a bent stick as if it were a bow,
and flare at the edges, light coming out of you.

You have the hunter's steady lope, ready to go
anywhere, risk anything on instinct,
and I need water, I need courage, I need rest.

I follow the blue flag and your hair,
your head a bright bird darting the Gorge
stooping now, and now, and now.

Potsherds, a fragment of rim, a handle-stump—
I bend to pick them up, sun high between walls
and my head hard in the heat.

I rattle my talismans, hoping to make you turn,
greasing the potter's thumbprint with my own.
How clear it all is, not a puff of air

until you punch my lungs with a look.
Hearts leap, I know, I felt it, I still feel it—
here in the dark, tracking you through sunlight.

Trespasser

Blood on her thighs from the long climb
through waist-high thorns from the sea.
Dust filming the blood, killing
reflection. Calmly she rolls her palms
in the paste, blunts highlights from her brow.

Dust on the olive as she leans her cheek
against smooth, nightsilvered bark.
Somewhere ahead, a crackling fire
spits and hangs heavy on the resiny air,
smoke and fat of a crackling rabbit.

Now she is moving like a gust of night,
long-legged, slow, upwind of the hunter.
She makes her eyes knife-slits.
She makes her breathing slow.
Her cold gaze settles on his neck.

Behind him the gully and the moon;
his lungs full of thyme, myrtle,
smoke of the fire and fat,
he rolls his shoulders, smug and content.
Lights a last cigarette before turning in.

Taverna on the Beach

Pomegranate thumbed open to reveal generations,
apple split to its white heart of flesh.
Ultramarine waters lap at stone,
lacing our days of light with drift of salt.
All night we cry and laugh and you
taste ash of apple on my skin—
delighting in apple, pomegranate, light and salt.

Deep in your veins you carry light and salt,
testing the fruit, breath pulsing under skin,
and unexpected urgencies push through—
laughter a remedy for the deep fault
under the streets, the reek of ancient stone.
All that the heart and mind can learn from flesh
piled in a rampart against the dead generations.

Running with the Immortals

Cobh is a world of silence as the sun breaks over the harbour
and the lighthouse at Roche's Point gleams, a torch
held out to the sky, to the eternal sea.
Something has woken me early, a drum tap, footfall echoing
in the empty streets. I'm at the open window. Too late—whoever it is
has already gone by, climbing the hill, steady and sure.

A clear mid-winter morning, frost on the slate beneath me,
tumble of roof and chimney down to the water. Already
the ferry tracking out towards Haulbowline, the world about its
    business
at this ungodly hour—and someone out there running the steep
blue streets. Hard work. Cobh is nothing if not uphill
and downhill, the uphill and downhill capital of Ireland.

On a morning like this, a girlchild out early would be thinking
    of glory—
the tall bowl of the stadium, black roar of the crowd, the red track,
the bend to the straight, the finish just visible through the haze.
Easy to dream of gold, olive-wreath, ceremony and applause,
the tricolour snapping to the arc-lights overhead, brass blaze
    of trumpets
—harder to rise to these winter mornings, these punishing hills,

yet somebody's up and out there, out there unseen and unknown,
climbing and falling with the street, breath raw in her throat,
pushing towards the sun, pushing against a wall of cold.
Bells from the Cathedral break over the waking town
while she keeps running on self-belief into the dawn,
an ordinary girl, head down, keeping time with her shadow.

I turn my face to the climbing sun, remembering another world,
a tall girl surging to the line. I want to find that child's soul and
    say:
Talent is not enough, belief is not enough in this world;
you must push out into the lonely place where it all falls away—
and then, if you're lucky and blessed, the friend at your shoulder,
keeping pace, will be long-legged clear-eyed Artemis herself.

Plato's Myth

In Plato's myth we are seated in a great cave,
numerous and murmurous there in the dark.
Across the cave mouth in a grave procession
pass men and women bearing statues; a dog barks
far off, cicadas chatter, the light is hard but kind
as each successive image prints on mind.

Myth, *muthos*, the breath of the real—
the world, ideally conceived, breathes and then sings.
Light is elsewhere, light is outside,
the world appears as the memory of things.

This is an autocrat's dream of order,
the poets banished, rule by the best.
My mind ponders, stirs itself to ask:
What statues? Made and shaped by whom?
And carried in what order?
Who briefed the crew to carry them? And,
what is the story we are to understand?

I prefer this: we stir there in the dark,
we rise and walk about, the talk starts up.
Somebody makes her way to the mouth of the cave,
stretches, steps out into first light.

Orpheus

The myth is a great bronze bell hung
in the stars and rafters of our story:
how Eurydice, fleet in the meadows,
was bit in the heel by a serpent
and tumbled headlong into death.

Perhaps death was a kind of glamour, Persephone
there before her with the Dark Lord was Queen
underground, remote, impersonal and cool—
so young, Eurydice, oak nymph, so easily led.
Not knowing her own best interests yet.

Imagine this: somewhere it was written that she might be saved,
that Orpheus, son of Apollo, walking the world
would wake it yet to overturn the underground's hard law,
and she knew this, or knew it vaguely,
but was already turned in a new fashion of forgetting.

And Orpheus, what did he know? Stones sang to his music
and lions lay down, mothers smiled coldly on him,
daughters grew pale and parched, he walked the world
in a flush of grief and power, lifted by the god's gift,
borne up by faith in love, convinced he could harrow Hell.

And down he went, to the amaze of all, down into the dark.
The words flew like daggers, bitter and cold:
—I came for you, even into Hell, to bring you home.
—You came for yourself, for glory and for the prize
of ever after pointing to the bride you brought back.

Perhaps she believed in his belief in love?
Maybe some light in his boyish face, some hope
that sparked the life she was by now letting fall away
caught fire in her breast? If you love me, she said,
trust me. Walk on ahead, but do not turn. A test.

And of course, he turned.

And she turned back.

I say he turned for love, afraid that will
might not overcome half-hearted doubt,
anxious to see he was not mistaken, anxious
to bring her on, to see her white foot following.
I say he believed that he knew best.

The myth glosses the moment like this: he gave his word
and broke it by turning round. She fell away.
What if it's otherwise? She stops to ask:
who is this, that he bargains for my fate?
He hears her scuff her foot, and halt.

And of course, he turns.

And she turns back.

What could he do after that? He courted death
with wine and cold abandon until, at his invitation,
the Maenads tore the song out of his throat,
they broke him limb from limb, they ate his heart
and drank his blood and spat him out.

There's something in all this about adult love,
it isn't a pretty story for the pubescent; the myth
is a warning bell and it shakes the walls
until plaster cracks and the bare bones stand out.
The Maenads did him a favour: he'd let her down.

When she walked off, he should have let her go,
not glamoured himself in fantasies of rescue,
himself as saviour; he could have shut up
and gone and done something useful, anything—
charmed lions, tidied the house, cooked for the poor.

Love is not love that false possession takes.
And love is not love that will not let love go.
We pity Eurydice, and our pity is misplaced:
she chose to accept what chance had offered her
and study her own pain. He could have waited.

Pity Orpheus, though he won't thank you for it.
It can't have been easy, standing there in the light,
watching her turn away, his love sure and true
but not enough. For what she needs to do, love
is never enough. It was time to let her go, to let her be.

The myth is silent on what came after,
on where he has been these long years—
there in some other dark, still working his baffled music
or long since come to light in his own silence.
I hope he made it back, and up, and out.

for Ciaran and Deirdre

Eurydice

High in the stars and rafters of our story
the myth hangs, a great bronze bell:
it tells how Orpheus, stricken by loss,
went down into the dark to save
his lost Eurydice from the pain of Hell.

Tripped up by Death she had gone down—
slow poison, the bite in the long grass,
bringing a kind of swoon, a sweet surrender.
Orpheus' journey a kind of rescue, his motive pure:
to save her from the dark, to bring her back.

But, what if we have it wrong? Imagine this:
Eurydice knew her heart, and knew it well;
she took to the dark and its possibilities,
a silence where she could make her soul,
an underworld for sure, the ground under ground.

And Orpheus, that charmer? Stones sang to his music
and lions lay down, mothers smiled fondly on him,
daughters flushed, he walked the world
so lightly, so sure of his gift and of himself—
and then she turns away, his one true love?

Night after night they argued, there in the dark.
The words flew like daggers, bitter and cold:
you left me, no I didn't, yes you did;
you never loved me, I did, and love you still
but this is my own way with myself. Now let me be.

I say he begged and argued, argued and sulked
until for peace at last, for quiet, for pity,

perhaps in hope, she bade him go, and stood behind.
Walk on, she said, trust me, walk on ahead into the light
but do not turn in doubt, do not look back.

And of course, he turned.

And she turned to stone.

They say he turned for love, afraid his will
might not be stronger than her fate,
anxious to see he was not mistaken, anxious
to bring her on, to see her firm on the path.
That his doubt broke his resolve, and she fell back.

But, what if we have it wrong? Imagine this:
against her better judgement she agreed
to follow him one more time into the life they'd shared;
crossing her fingers she promised herself—
if he doesn't turn, he'll have understood. He'll wait.

And of course, he turns.

And she turns to stone.

The Maenads tore the song out of his throat,
they broke him limb from limb, they ate his heart
and drank his blood and spat him out.
So much for charm: he believed her glamoured
but they knew better. She chose herself.

There's something ugly and terrible in this:
it isn't a pretty story for teenage lovers, the myth
is a warning bell and it shakes the walls
until plaster cracks and the bare bones stand out.
The Maenads got it right: he let her down.

When she was taken, he should have let her go,
not wound himself into fantasies of rescue,
himself as saviour; he should have shut up
and gone and done something useful, anything—
charmed lions, tidied the house, cooked for the poor.

Love is not love that false possession takes.
And love is not love that will not let love go.
We pity Orpheus, and our pity is misplaced:
he should have let her be to unweave her own soul
and suffer her fated pain. He should have waited.

Pity Eurydice, though she won't thank you for it.
It can't have been easy, standing there like a stone
watching him stumble away, his love sure and true
but not enough. For what she needs to do, love
is never enough. It was time to let her go, to let her be.

The myth is silent on what came after,
on where she has been these long years—
there in the dark, still working her soul
or long since come to light in her own silence.
I hope she made it back, and up, and out.

for Deirdre and Ciaran

28

Return to Hania

Here I am come to Hania again
but now, suddenly, full of years.
The bronze girls go by in pairs,
almost they walk through me.

Am I a ghost in this evening air?

This morning I woke in Piraeus to catch the boat,
and thought as I dressed of that other ferry
I must take before long. Amazed, I hung
between one mouthful of coffee and the next.

Old bones, dear beating heart,
how many laughing women
once laid their faces to that pulse—
some are already gone to dust, others
are mysteries now, mothers, grandmothers!

It has not been what we expected.

It beggars breath to speak of it; such lives
we have led, who were lithe as the bronze girls
or the quick young men who throng the square,
eternity in their every breath and glance.
I thought my life a catalogue of loss—
now, without meaning to, I see it all as gain;
I am dizzy with hope, stunned—so much laughter
and love, such joy come round again!

Figure from the Archaic

Time for the unquiet dead to have their say.
I lay my weapons down, I walk away.

Ithaca

When you set out from Ithaca again,
let it be autumn, early, the plane leaves falling as you go,
for spring would shake you with its quickening,
its whispers of youth.

You will have earned the road down to the harbour,
duty discharged, your toll of labour paid,
the house four-square, your son in the full of fatherhood,
his mother, your long-beloved, gone to the shades.

Walk by the doorways, do not look left or right,
do not inhale the woodsmoke,
the shy glow of the young girls,
the resin and pine of home.
Stand there and hold their gaze,
they have been good neighbours.

Plank fitted to plank, slow work and sure,
the mast straight as your back.
Water and wine, oil, salt and bread.
Take a hand in yours for luck.

Cast off the lines without a backward glance
and sheet in the sail.
There will be harbours, shelter from weather;
there will be long empty passages far from land.
There may be love or kindness, do not count on this
but allow for the possibility.
Be ready for storms.

When you take leave of Ithaca, round to the south
then strike far down for Circe, Calypso,
what you remember, what you must keep in mind.
Trust to your course, long since laid down for you.
There was never any question of turning back.
All those who came the journey with you,
those who fell to the flash of bronze,
those who turned away into other fates,
are long gathered to asphodel and dust.
You will go uncompanioned, but go you must

There will be time in the long days and nights,
stunned by the sun or driven by the stars,
to unwind your spool of life.
You will learn again what you always knew—
the wind sweeps everything away.

When you set out from Ithaca again,
you will not need to ask where you are going.
Give every day your full, reflective attention—
the rise and flash of the swell on your beam,
the lift into small harbours—
and do not forget Ithaca, keep Ithaca in your mind.
All that it was and is, and will be without you.

Be grateful for where you have been,
for those who kept to your side,
those who strode out ahead of you
or stood back and watched you sail away.
Be grateful for kindness in the perfumed dark
but sooner or later you will sail out again.

Some morning, some clear night,
you will come to the Pillars of Hercules.
Sail through if you wish. You are free to turn back.
Go forward on deck, lay your hand on the mast,
hear the wind in its dipping branch.
Now you are free of home and journeying,
rocked on the cusp of tides.
Ithaca is before you, Ithaca is behind you.
Man is born homeless, and shaped for the sea.
You must do what is best.

for Leonard Cohen

ISLANDS

Honey Yoghurt

Sea blue on the chairs and table,
the sun faded shutters, the taverna door behind me.
A concrete platform by the sea, frayed yellow rope
to a fishing boat bumping softly against smooth rock.
I am adrift in time, breakfasting here while you sleep
in a cool cave of dark, the storm gone over.

They bring me fruit—a nectarine, a peach—more coffee.
Odysseus puts a hand on my shoulder, I look up but he is staring
out to sea, a ferry pushing along the horizon, someone
swimming straight out from shore, as if never to return.
Presently I walk back the track with breakfast on a tray.
You step out of the shower as I stoop through the doorway—
your skin so brown, the towel, your sudden smile, so very white.

Inland

Cicadas drizzling through the marsh bamboo,
a bend in the road; a crescent of white dust
laid on the red earth, a full stop in shade.
Buzz of a three-wheeler, far off up the mountain.

A blank plaque of heat, the pewter sea.
An oiled sheet of tin, the grey-blue sky.

Here is the perfect place for grief
to lie coiled in ambush.
I have seen such places in the world before.
I turn and make my way back towards the beach.

A Farm on the Edge of Ocean

A farm on the edge of ocean.
Close-cropped grass,
musk of some resiny herb, a few low thorns,
stone and dry red earth, the sea beneath.

Blue house under stark pines,
a dog in the doorway barking and barking
until the vaulted sky booms back
and the downpour black is scythed through by light.

I scramble downhill for shelter,
rock to rock, fork-legged, antic,
scattering thin sheep.
The fear so immediate, striking deep.

Alexandros

A woman calls, Alexandros! Alexandros!
Silence flashes through the cavernous market.
A boy comes backlit through the entrance arch,
a carefree, sunny child, all smiles and puppy fat.
Nevertheless we search his eyes as he ambles past,
we who have seen tyrants in their youth before now.

Cross-Country Bus

A small town on the road through the hills.
I forget where we were coming from, forget
where we were going. The bus slowed
at a slur in the houses, a break in the wall,
and you leaned in against me. Hot, dust billowing.
Downslope then, jostled and conscious of bodies,
rosaries banging against the windscreen,
meat in the driver's arms as he wrestled the wheel.

A small town on the road through the hills,
I have never forgotten it.

A crone in a black headscarf looked up at us,
shook her fist, tilted her head, giggled.

You elbowed me and I made a severe face
at you, at the old woman. The whole bus started
laughing, and comedy ripped down the crooked
street like a string of fire crackers. The driver
dropped a gear and we growled on, buoyant
and close to bursting into song.

Nikos

Every day he swims straight out from shore.
A mile out. A mile back.
Every day Angela sits here and watches.
Fifty years of this.
As a parting gift, I leave her my binoculars.
She is politely puzzled, mild.
To watch him drown, I say.
A smile, a long slow smile.
She lifts her chin. He laughs, he turns away.

Spirits

Yannis shouldn't drink in the afternoon,
it makes him dull and querulous, morose like me:

What do I care about Actaeon in your eyes,
this cultural tourism? Tell me about Ireland,
what you see when you walk the streets,
what ghosts prompt your murders, what shades
your executioners send down out of daylight?
You have your poor and your policemen,
your crime and politics and lawyers—
affliction is real, write about that.

He's right, I think, he has a point...

and Artemis bumps the table, T-shirt and blue jeans,
a diamond glinting in one ear, phone to the other.
She stalks past, imperious and aloof,
radiant in her first flush of immortality.

for Socrates Kabouropoulos

Survivor

Athenian lawyer, on holiday here in the islands.
I offer a cigarette, he pours two more brandies.
The waiter is scattering bread on the water,
we sit on in the lone light left burning.

The subject is civil war; we have been talking
about my poor country, he asks me to explain
'affable irregular' when, in a lucid lurch of trust,
I ask how it was here, under the Colonels?

He holds my eyes with his, he makes a fist.
Veteran and stern, the ring finger missing.

After the Tourists Have Gone Home

We sit under the awning, backs to the wall.
Eleni brings coffee and water, our usual.
The tourists float past and around us,
bright-coloured fish in schools.
Five minutes, the bakery will open.
Rattle of heavy chain, the ferry is in.
Costas is putting out papers, a rack of postcards.
Eyes hooded, you smile to yourself
watching it all start up again.

Eleni, what does the island do in winter?
She bursts out laughing. Do? The men go to sea.
It is quiet, you know. Mostly adultery.

Under a Blue and White Striped Awning

That time between the heat of day and evening,
when cats thread between rickety chairs
and the waiters are gossiping, smoking at the bar.

Maria is opening the minimarket door, the lock stiff
as ever; she nods to you, we have been here that long,
and you wave back.

We'll need bread, grapes, water,
but now we need coffee. *Zesto, me gala.*

Giorgos embraces an older man in a pressed shirt, grey straw hat,
offers his hand gravely to the man's lithe companion.
The heaven Cavafy dreamed of, love acknowledged.

Young Love

We've been watching them for the past half-hour,
everyone has been watching them,
the young Americans in their whirlwind of despair.
Whatever picked them up in the world
and held them together is no longer enough—
it is the end of the dream,
                          the end of love,
                                     the end of the world.

The afternoon ferry bangs in, the ramp slams down,
everything now is bustle and heavy metal,
trucks roaring down the ramp, trucks roaring up,
a tidal wave of grannies and locals and scooters
sweeping in and out.

What will they do, we ask, stay or go?

Nobody here in the cafeneion
has drawn a breath for five minutes
when she grabs her impossibly heavy
rucksack and drags it aboard
without a backward glance.

He stands there, stone, a monument to heartbreak.

The siren blares, hawsers splash in the water,
the ramp drags over the hot concrete, a high metal screech
and then there is water between ramp and jetty,
the gap opening, opening...

We don't cheer the boy when he takes a running jump,
we cheer Dimitrios, Maria's boy in his crisp white shirt,
his first job as a man, Dimitrios
who hangs from the chain at the ramp's edge
and times the roar perfectly, his hand outstretched.
Dimitrios, nineteen himself, a believer in love
and wiser than us, with our stopped hearts,
our misplaced pity for the young.

Bread Dipped in Olive Oil and Salt

Bread dipped in olive oil and salt,
a glass of rough dry white.

A table beside the evening sea
where you sit shelling pistachios,
flicking the next open with the half-
shell of the last, story opening story,
on down to the sandy end of time.

The stars coming out on the life that I call mine

Morning in the Cafeneion

I sit in the cafeneion with the old men
nursing a thick dark coffee and a book.
Sometimes I hear a soft collective sigh
and turn to the open window for a look.
It's always a surprise what's passing by,
sometimes a girl, of course, with rich black hair,
a solemn, unheeding princess, but it can be
a warrior matron stepping proud or a loud
and beautiful shambolic drunk, heart full of joy.
Once one of those dark-eyed immortal boys.

Visitors

A boat comes nosing in to the quay,
steady and sure, trim and slow.
I stand up and gesture for the bowline.
Small, dark, she smiles—the line
comes neatcoiled through the air.
Efharisto. Ná h-abair, fáilte.
A hand on the rail, she stares.

She sees a greyhaired man,
tanned and stocky, a surprise.
I make them fast, toss back the end of line.
He has come forward, stands there,
a hand on her waist, quizzical.
I jerk my chin at the tricolour
snug to the spreader. No need to say more.
Like myself, they are on a break from history,
the softvoiced, troubled language of our tribe.
I turn away, they turn away. Enough for now.

Journey's End

The house of the winds levelled,
waist-high dry grass, dust,
goat droppings, leaves.
Here, says the local teacher,
they found a bronze cauldron—
or was it here?
His hand rises, he lets it fall.
What does it matter, here or over there?

We both look away.
A great weight of heat and light,
flat clang of a bell.
And this is what he fought through for—
home. This empty place.

Nike

This girl can tell you how much Nikes cost,
but doesn't know who Nike is, or was.

Better dead than out of fashion—Oscar Wilde
would understand this pouting anxious child,

her grim determination to fit in,
to add her moped's wasp-roar to the din

of daily life in all its dusty charm,
impress the boys who go by arm-in-arm.

Winged victories were carved for girls like her,
to make them fleet of foot and never tire;

The goddess on her plinth above the square
is wall-eyed, blank—as if not really there.

Impermanent Things

That rock off Fourni, for instance, today it's half as close
as yesterday, tomorrow perhaps it will have sailed back.
Maybe Hektor is right, it's a trick of light
and water in the air. The islands don't move at all,
he says, perched on his chair outside the last taverna.

I'm not so sure. I asked Maria about Hektor today.
Him? she said, him? Left school in 1963, sells fish
and sits outside that place when the shop is shut.
Since 1963, imagine, at home or in the shop, or in that chair.
Never been anywhere, Hektor. Don't listen to him.

The French Bee-Keeper

He's counting his coins into a scuffed small purse,
I buy him a coffee, he nods to you and smiles.
He sleeps in caves, abandoned houses;
at night sometimes, he says, he lights a fire;
mostly he isn't cold, or hungry, or lonely.
People don't notice, he says, if I keep myself quiet.

People don't notice, he says, I sleep in a house
one day, two, I move on. I find letters, sometimes
old clothes, newspapers from the 1950s. He wonders,
he says, where the people went. America, I say,
those are their children you see in the cafés, back
to the island as tourists, their Greek halting and slow.

Last night, I say, in that restaurant, a girl with her nose pierced,
head nodding to her i-pod, accent nasal New England—
a shawled granny went by, came back, stood, said:
"Your mother sat beside me, daughter of Dymas".

I'm a bee-keeper, he says, I don't understand.
It's an island, I say; believe me, they notice you.

Nisos Ikaria

Green fastness, high and sheer,
tall pines and clear air,
red earth & light-split rock,
cicadas ticking like a clock.

In deep winter when the rain
beats against the windowpane
we sleep as two about to die
and spell the future, you and I.

Two figures walk that gravel beach
their heads inclined, each speaks to each
in words that come from otherwhere—
we make such lucid sense, my dear.

On that small island where we go
by night to watch the starry show
we dance as lovers used to dance
in a slow, stately, gravid trance.

The rain beats on the windowpane,
we lie beneath those pines again,
we watch the moon and stars roll past,
reading the sky, at ease at last.

Over Delphi

The jet banked left over Delphi
and there I was, looking down
at the deep-cleft gorge,
the ridge with its flat pine crown,
a tumbled array of temples,
a crowd struck dumb
as engines thundered across heaven
and a bright god circled.

You may prefer to say, a tourist looked up
at the voice of Zeus, the flash of Hermes' wing—
here is that still inviolate place
where we choose what we sing.

SAPPHO'S DAUGHTER

for Katerina Anghelaki Rooke

PROLOGOS

A red ball bounces in the scribble of surf,
heel-deep in shingle a child watches
and I watch the child, her father bending
to scoop handfuls of water into the air.

Propped on my elbows I scan the crescent bay,
the rock promontory at either tip
shattered by light, the sea almost perfectly still.
The white sky is holding its breath.

Into the picture comes the plump caique that
brought us here this morning, the boy
at her forepeak watching for swimmers as
she noses out, helms over to go north.

The hum of the town behind us, the rasp
and the roar of scooters, deep bray of the
over-the-mountain bus. Naked beside me,
you nuzzle my forearm, sigh and turn over.

To lie naked under the sun beside the sea,
how simple and beautiful that is. I feel the thought
turn over in your mind, a catspaw breeze
cuffing the olives behind us. *We are so close.*

So far, so good. All this I remember, can call up
almost without effort. What's next is difficult.
I lay back, I remember this, and a phrase emerged,
stood clear of the drowse and hum—

It was no dream, I lay broad waking. I moved
to supply the words before or after, but a dull weight
pressed on my chest and a vacuum came in my
breathing. I could not shift or speak
and then he spoke,
and this is what I heard:

I saw an island from our painted ship
a chasm opening,
a sudden splitting down to the earth's core.

The sea was navy blue around our ship
while at the island's edge it boiled grey-white.
A puff of smoke, domestic almost, climbed
and grew tall as Mount Ida—

then groves of young timber tumbled in,
the chasm darkening as the roar reached us.
Suddenly it was all business, the crew jabbering
and leaping from their oars, the steersman
roaring at them to be still,
the captain, a philosopher, stroking his beard.

Me, I knew the next thing was a tidal wave.
It reached us seconds later. I had a rope
twice round the mast, once round my arm,
it bit my wrist as I stood on my head and
swallowed water but it held, it held.
Not so the ship, smashed under in seconds.

Spewing water like a Hania dolphin
I surfaced and found myself alone.
The mast and a few boards were all that survived
of our Athenian glory, the crew,
slavemaster, captain all gone under.
I hope Poseidon was kind to them. He was kind to me.
Rock floated on water, the air was thick with ash.
I married a spar for two days and nights
before a trader scavenging the flotsam raked me in.
Late summer to dead of winter
I made up chart and course,
found them by half-instinct

port after port where gold and fish
brought in some profit.
Before they'd cut my throat for luck I jumped ship
for passage to Lesvos on a roving scout.
I've always known when my luck was running out.

Fetched up in Sigri, Calypso took me in,
a baker's daughter, father dead, the business her own.

Snug to the ovens I slept, and walked by day
as quiet a shore as ever a man had found.
At night the sound of bells as sheep moved pasture
carried across the bay to the sleeping island
where trees were cast in stone and no leaf stirred.

The air was calm in that place,
the people slow and sure.
I grew in confidence, content
my fate should never find me out.

Sappho unmade me, Eressan Sappho,
swarth, surefooted, canny.
I'd taken a day's turn with a neighbour,
churning the oars like an old salt
while he hauled nets and grumbled
the stark length of coast to Skala Eressou.
I think now he'd intended to pay me
in callouses for the long nights
I'd amazed his wife in tales of adventure.

Often that hot Spring day
I'd seen him choke a grin

as I surveyed the map of blisters
spreading across my palms.
He had a low mind and a weak chin.

I needed wine by the bucket when we landed,
sought out the darkest taverna I could find.
Before I'd sunk a cup she had found my mind.

You know those mornings on Rethymnon's lagoon
when the gold fog slips fingers across the bay,
and birds dart in and out of view
like stray notes on a lyre?
It was like that, I felt the fingers of her mind
spreading to find me out,
steadying, locking on.
I was a dolphin as the net closed in,
felt every mesh and knot along
the bumps standing on my hide.

Never went fish or fowl so willingly
to the net. I pushed the jug away
(a cup fell, and did not break)
and walked out in the full stream
of some story just begun.
The sun was low along the shore
and that's how I saw her first,
an outline against the father of all thirst.

Singing she was, of islands great and small,
her hands behind her back, her eyes cast down.
Like a bashful girl, stubbing her toe in sand,
radiant and invisible all at once.

I stood there speechless as she came on,
my eyes on her form against the sun,
my mind in torment.

She passed me without a glance,
I thought a spear had found me,
turning my guts like lamb upon a spit.
But the fire in my belly was nothing
against the fire in my mind.
Artemis walked, I swear, Eressos' shore.

Nothing could hold me, nothing
could turn me back. I followed
where her mind pulled like a strong net of shades,
back through the village where my Sigrian friend
pressed his hand over his eyes, refusing to see.
I wanted to shout, you bastard, grab hold of me,
pull me back, but the power wasn't there, or the will.
I had found my course and was fated to follow,
my back firm to the bright shield of the sun.

> Ash of Hephaestos the bright dust
> Green of Demeter the vine and squash,
> The path a pale snake through the olives
> As he treads my wake.
>
> I am a peeled wand in bright afternoon,
> A green thing, quick with life.
> Lives are dust beneath my sandal,
> Aeons funnelling to the snake.

I am a mast and a green boat,
I am the sea and the ship's course,
I am the snake a boat inscribes on water.

She never looked back once,
or saw I was there for all I knew,
but when we came to her house
an old woman stood in the gateway,
barred my path.
I watched as her mistress
ran to scoop an infant
from excited shade, to calm
with a downturned palm
a leaping dog. Without a backward look
she walked towards singing voices,
girls' voices, a chorus in the trees,
but the child's look held me,
and the old woman's.

And I who had dared the African sun
stood there as if my tongue had taken root,
as if Crete had never fired my giddy blood.
The crone (might have been Achilles' twin,
you know what I mean) nodded me once
to the side, the farmyard,
and damn me if I didn't slope after,
a dog bidden at midday to lap water.

I cut wood. I drew hay from the small meadow,
fed and tended goats. I built walls, re-roofed outhouses,
shook out the black nets for olives, hoed

squash and bean and vine and every manner of thing.
All day and every day I watched for her,
listened to hear her voice above all others
ring out through the green shade,
rising above the chorus like a sparrow rising
    from an eagle's back
when he has climbed to the height.

At night I'd wash, watch stars dusting the heavens
as the day's dirt fell with water to the ground.
I thought the cicadas were stars of grit
rubbing in my brain. I hoped the night wind
would cool me, that the rough wine
would bring on sleep. In this at least
I was lucky, I slept without dreams.

    He came as I saw he would, lithe as
        a fisherman, cursing the oars.
    The eye on the prow calming the wave,
        his man at the helm
    knotting old nets. The sun on his
        shoulder as the dream had foretold.
    I sent a young singing bird down to the
        beach, she watched where he went.
    When I knew he had taken a mouthful of
        wine, I closed up my eyes,
    went deep for the steadying vision and
        called up the song.

    I sent myself walking the sand, winding
        him down to the deep
    where the fish in red armour walk slowly

the rock and the weed.
When I felt the tide turn I cast, caught
him and hauled on the net.

Sun between shoulderblades turned me
to ghost as I passed by his eyes,
I felt his heart leap in my breast like a
fish in a pool but I passed,
when I turned for the homeplace I heard
his foot slap in my dust.

That was the drumbeat my heart's song
had waited the years for.
He flared at my heels like a fire, dreams
like a torrent I meant
to tame, channel and feed to my vines
pouring onto his feet.

When I passed through the gate I faltered
and wanted to turn
but a child called in her fright where the
dog had grown bold.
I watched in the bronze of her eyes as I
went to the house:
my mother had measured him, fixed on
his station and place.

I had to teach my singing birds new
measure and grace,
I had to guard my look and thought,
make my face
mask of the moon, watch myself, ward
myself

in word and gesture. My lovers at night
    became troubled
and sad, turning under my hand like fish
    in dark water.
I watched until the stars had dusted the
    full grapes,
keeping his dreams from him the better
    to take his body.

Rain had been falling all the afternoon
after a morning bright with foreign ships.
They'd landed, ten or more, galleys & troopships
for Chios, they say, lean and businesslike.
I watched from one of my groves; they just took
on water, ignoring the village, the women,
made a quick offering on the beach at noon
and then shoved off. They rounded
the headland in good order, making south,
black rain followed them in from the north.

I had become a husbandman, my vines
and green things more important to me
than flash of bronze in battle or dice on deck.
I felt no loss as they pulled away,
I had done with the sea, that graveyard of wrecks.
But Sappho, my lady, had not done with me.

Rain had been falling all the afternoon
and I was content to watch it fall.
Terracing caught and caved it until the pools
were brimming full, then sluices let if fall

in steps and gradients to the lower valley.
I could admire it as a work of art,
this husbanding and doling out of water.
Under the canopy of my simple house I watched
until the brimming fall and fill of it brought desire
welling through my veins.

She is a voice among voices
a white bird in the olive grove
dust at the wind's heel on a path.

The face of her mother's house was shut against me,
her singing school sheltering under a wing of silence.
In the dip between our houses the draggled olives
muttered and swung in gust and gap of rain.

She is a lamp in a dark house at noon
the promised smell of linen
a jar of oil in a cool cellar

Nobody shifted in the fields or in the village below.
Nothing warmblooded stirred in the weeds,
I lifted the wineskin but had no taste for it, let it fall.

She is the silence after song
the crust cracking on new bread
salt on sunwarm boards

The rain stopped and black night fell early.

Oh light the lamps and sweep the floor,
bind olive and oak to the lintel,
light the lamps and sweep the floor
let flute with voices play.
Over the threshold he will come
with owl in the swaying bush outside
and I will tap on the goatskin drum
to guide his way.
Over the sea the full moon swings
and the lamp in the wind,
oak and olive frame the door
and Sappho would be lone no more,
let the music play, the hymn for a child.

Such music.
I though my heart would stop.
I lifted my hand to shoulder-height, let it fall.
I blew on my flame, it swayed,
leaned all the way over
and sprung back.
I stripped and walked outside,
doused myself over and over,
bucket after bucket until the rain-butt
was empty that had been brimming.
The music would not stop.

Someone flung out an abrupt net of stars.
The drenched earth flooded the air
with lemon, olive, acacia, grape and thyme.
I thought my heart would never stop
until it had burst from my chest,
the drumming that had been the drumming of rain

now pounding in my blood,
beating from ear to ear, from wall to wall,
I should say, of some great echoing cave.
Every muscle, sinew and nerve in me
straightened and sang like fine rope rigging
and my bones hummed with the strain of it,
I was a ship fit for the plunge and voyage out.

I gathered my things.
A few clothes, my knife,
the wineskin. A cloak
that her mother had given
with rough grace, the wool
soft, close-woven, fine.
Everything there that was mine.

The gardens parted at my coming,
the vines and squash, the heavy grapes
and the olives I had tended
with such devotion rolled back
and away from me like waves of the sea.
There was a single light
high up in the sleeping house,
oak and olive over the door,
a dull shine on the bare boards
and silence everywhere, deep as the night.

I heard him come through garden
       and grove
the fall of his foot in the dust,
the sound of each breath.

I wound the song in, breathing
soft, easy and slow, taking care
not to break the thread.

My dove of night, I called him,
my owl and my bull,
pulse of my beating heart.

My mountain torrent, I called him,
my dolphin, my goat,
my torment, my keener.

Come closer, come close if you dare
and be good if you can, first
and last man.

Fire to my womb, crusher of breath,
come sing the one song
of my house; give me a daughter.

I can see now I was had.
Laugh and I'll laugh with you.
Fattened and toughened
and kept on a leash
like a horse or a bull,
my right pride and my skills
at nought, an enchanted gardener,
a fool for love.
I was many things then
before and since but I swear
by the wind of death,
I swear by the springs of Hyperion

and the groves of Ida
if I had known then what I knew after
I'd still have stepped over that threshold,
climbed those stairs, pushed in that door
and crossed that wide wood floor
with as firm a step as ever a man has made.

Oh lightning sweet and rough
wave of the south
wind of the north.
Oh lightning sweet and rough
I am scorched in the fire
though my blood does not burn
drowned in the sea
and breathing yet.
Oh lightning sweet and deep
my feet are on fire,
my womb is a cave of ocean
and Poseidon, Poseidon
beats on its walls in flood.
    Oh the white dust,
the path through the murmuring grove,
my honey, my sweet of evening,
my sleep, my sleep by the sea.

The moon made a path of silver and she lay
athwart it, aslant on the great bed, uncovered.
My lungs were huge, I breathed hard and slow
as I walked and walked to her, I thought the room
enchanted, leagues wide and deep.

I thought a sparrow skittered, below me in the house,
it was a flick of a thing, a fever of seconds, a stone
falling and its taste a moment in my mouth.

Her tongue tasted of apples, of sweet yellow wine,
her breasts yielding and sure, her thigh slender
and muscular twined around mine.
She had the strongest back I had ever bucked
and fought, her hips ground me like a wrestler's
and her lips were music mouthing into mine.
I spent in a night what flesh I'd made all summer,
she matched me cry for cry
and wept as women do, when dawn
shook birds awake outside, and I wept too.

There was a ship, Athenian trader, on the beach.
She walked me through the gardens I'd made,
I knew she was remaking them in her mind as we walked.
Her singing birds were stirring behind in the courtyard,
her mother appeared at a bend, embraced me,
pinched my arse for luck and laughed for the first time,
and I laughed too. A grimace, no more. I was sore
in every muscle, crushed and bruised and drained
but I walked with back erect, head up, spring in my step,
you know the drill. I can see it still in my mind's eye,
the crescent of beach beneath us, the fall of her land
away down to the sea. There she took leave of me
with a single kiss, I was branded and dismissed.

Ash of Hephaestos the bright dust,
Green of Demeter the vine and squash,
The path a pale snake through the olives
As he trod my wake.

I am a peeled wand in bright afternoon,
A green thing, quick with life.
Lives are dust beneath my sandal,
Aeons funnelling to the snake.

He was a mast and a green boat,
I was the sea and the ship's course,
He was the snake a boat inscribes on water
And I am the white gull now, ghosting his wake.

Come bees and bring me honey
Come stream and channel, garden my land
Come sun and moon and light me,
Bring me a golden daughter to my hand.

Well there it is, I was first and last and only.
It starts with an island foundering in the wide sea
and it never ends. I was blessed and cast down,
cast out and found again, brought home but not for good.
Last night I dreamed I had a daughter,
but I dreamed of bread and gold, too.
This happened me, just as I tell you
and nobody knows what may happen yet.
Nobody knows what may happen in this life.

EPILOGOS

An engine boomed and the world came crashing back
as a jet flicked in the sky, banked over, thundered
away to sea. You started there beside me,
grabbed at my arm and stared at the sudden bay.

I thought you'd seen him, just before he faded,
but there was no distance in your look.
I felt shook, troubled and far away, thought better
of talking about it, halted, inadequate, gruff

until you said "sometimes here in the islands it's as if
time is full, full, and the dead reborn."
Then you heard what you'd said, fell silent. I said
"Nobody knows what may happen in this life".

NOTES

'Begin, Begin Again' (p.11)
St. 3: *Kali mera.* Gr. Good morning
St. 4: *Torann na dtonn le sleasaibh na long*
ag tarraingt go teann 'n ár gceann fé sheol.
Ir. Thunder of waves on the hull of the ship
pulling straight towards us under sail
Measaim gur súbhach don Mhumhain an fhuaim...
Ir. This is a joyful sound for Munster...

The lines in Irish are from the song Rosc Catha Na
Mumhan, The Battle Hymn Of Munster

'Under a Blue and White Striped Awning' (p. 46)
St. 3 *Zesto, me gala.* Gr. Hot, with milk.

'Visitors' (p. 51)
St. 1 *Efharisto.* Gr. Thank you.
Ná h-abair, fáilte.
Ir. Don't mention it, (you are) welcome.

'Journey's End' (p. 52)
"The house of the winds" refers to Odysseus' home on
the island of Ithaca.

Lightning Source UK Ltd.
Milton Keynes UK
UKOW041527110613

212081UK00001B/110/P

VAT for Solicitors

VAT for Solicitors

John Phelps LL.B

Julian Gizzi M.A.

Partners, Beachcroft Stanleys

Butterworths
London, Dublin & Edinburgh
1993

United Kingdom	Butterworth & Co (Publishers) Ltd, 88 Kingsway, LONDON WC2B 6AB and 4 Hill Street, EDINBURGH EH2 3JZ
Australia	Reed International Books Australia Pty Ltd, SYDNEY, MELBOURNE, BRISBANE, ADELAIDE, PERTH, CANBERRA and HOBART
Belgium	Butterworth & Co Publishers, BRUSSELS
Canada	Butterworths Canada Ltd, TORONTO and VANCOUVER
Ireland	Butterworth (Ireland) Ltd, DUBLIN
Malaysia	Malayan Law Journal Sdn Bhd, KUALA LUMPUR
New Zealand	Butterworths of New Zealand Ltd, WELLINGTON and AUCKLAND
Puerto Rico	Equity de Puerto Rico, Inc, HATO REY
Singapore	Malayan Law Journal Pte Ltd, SINGAPORE
USA	Butterworth Legal Publishers, AUSTIN, Texas; BOSTON, Massachusetts; CLEARWATER, Florida (D & S Publishers); ORFORD, New Hampshire (Equity Publishing); ST PAUL, Minnesota; and SEATTLE, Washington

A CIP Catalogue record for this book is available from the British Library

ISBN 0 406 02008 6

Typeset by BP Integraphics Ltd, Bath, Avon
Printed and bound in Great Britain by Mackays of Chatham PLC, Chatham, Kent

Preface

Several years have passed since the first edition of *Solicitors and VAT*. This new edition, published under the new title *VAT for Solicitors* takes account of the new procedures made necessary by the Solicitors' Accounts Rules 1991 and the completion of the Single Market. In addition, we have taken the opportunity to revise the structure of the book and to expand its coverage.

In spite of this, we hope we have not lost sight of what this book was originally intended to be and how we intended it to be used: a practical guide to be kept by your side to provide ready answers to the VAT questions which arise every time you draw a cheque, deliver an invoice or receive a remittance.

We should like to thank Butterworths staff for their support and patience, our colleagues Coby Van Wijk, Dalla Jenney, Gemma Clark and Christine Riddle for their help with research and Julie Sharman and Louise Wöbcke for typing the manuscript.

20 Furnival Street,   John Phelps
London EC4A 1BN   Julian Gizzi
March 1993

Contents

Appendices

Abbreviations

VAT	Value Added Tax
VATA 1983	Value Added Tax Act 1983
the General Regulations	The Value Added Tax (General) Regulations 1985
the VAT Guide	Customs & Excise Notice No 700 (1 August 1991)

In this book, references to the United Kingdom are to be construed as including references to the Isle of Man.

I Introduction

To some solicitors, VAT is a fascinating subject. To others, probably the majority, it is a subject which they would rather leave to accountants. To all, an understanding of the subject, at least insofar as it impinges upon their own practice, is essential.

This book addresses only those aspects of VAT which affect you in the conduct of your practice. Some grasp of the way in which VAT works is necessary, however, and the next chapter explains the fundamental terms and concepts.

Before sending out any invoice, one of the questions which you must ask yourself is whether you should charge VAT on your fees. The completion of the Single Market on 1 January 1993 has led to changes in this area as it has in other aspects of carrying on business in the EC. The old zero-rating regime for the supply of services abroad has gone and the new rules are explained in Chapter III. New invoicing requirements have also been introduced and these are covered in Chapter VI.

'When is a disbursement not a disbursement for VAT purposes?' is a question which remains as difficult as it was when we wrote the first edition of this book. The debate which has recently taken place in the legal press about the VAT treatment of telegraphic transfer fees emphasises the need for greater clarification in this area. In Chapter IV, we have sought to explain the principles involved in such a way as to simplify the identification and treatment of the various types of payment you may make in the course of acting for your client.

The Solicitors' Accounts Rules 1991 prohibit you from paying into your office account remittances received in respect of unpaid Counsel's fees. Unless care is taken, you may find yourself in breach of the Rules or unable to recover the VAT. You should be able to avoid these traps by following the procedures set out in Chapter V. Chapter V also deals with the requirement to invoice yourself in respect of certain supplies you receive from abroad.

Another topic which tends to cause problems within the profession is in regard to the payment of a solicitor's fees by someone other than his client. To whom should you address your invoice in these circumstances? To whom should you send it? Who should pay the VAT? Who is entitled to treat the VAT as his input tax? The answers to these and other related questions are provided in Chapter VII.

Until 1989 it was only possible to obtain relief from VAT on bad debts in cases where your client became formally insolvent. The new, more relaxed rules are summarised in Chapter VIII.

II Glossary of terms and concepts

VAT
A tax which is 'charged on any supply of goods or services made in the United Kingdom where it is a taxable supply made by a taxable person in the course or furtherance of any business carried on by him' (VATA 1983, section 2(1)).

Taxable person
A person who is, or is required to be, registered for VAT (VATA 1983, section 2C(1)).

In other words he will be a taxable person if:

(i) the value of his taxable supplies exceeds the limits set out in VATA 1983, Schedule 1 (as amended from time to time) and he has registered under VATA 1983; or

(ii) the value of his taxable supplies exceeds those statutory limits, but he has failed so to register; or

(iii) the value of his taxable supplies does not exceed the statutory limits, but he has chosen so to register.

Supply
A supply of goods or services made in either case for a consideration. VATA

3

1983, Schedule 2 sets out various matters to be treated as supplies and provides for instance that:

(i) the grant, assignment or surrender of a major interest in land (ie the sale of a freehold or the grant of a lease for a term of more than 21 years) is a supply of goods (paragraph 4);

(ii) a gift of goods worth more than £10 by a person carrying on a business is a supply of goods (paragraph 5(1));

(iii) where business goods are put to private use (whether or not for a consideration) that is a supply of services (paragraph 5(3)).

Taxable supply   A supply made in the United Kingdom, other than an exempt supply (VATA 1983, section 2(2)). For VAT to be chargeable the taxable supply must be made by a taxable person in the course or furtherance of any business carried on by him. At present a taxable supply is either a zero-rated supply or a standard-rated supply.

Exempt supply   A supply of a description for the time being specified in VATA 1983, Schedule 6 (eg postal services) (VATA 1983, section 17(1)).

Zero-rated supply   A taxable supply of a description for the time being specified in VATA 1983, Schedule 5 (eg books, certain international services) (VATA 1983, section 16(2)).

Standard-rated supply

A taxable supply, not being a zero-rated supply, which, if made by a taxable person in the course or furtherance of any business carried on by him, will be chargeable to VAT at the standard rate (currently 17.5%).

Outside the scope of VAT

A supply is outside the scope of VAT if it is not or is not deemed to be made in the United Kingdom by a taxable person in the course or furtherance of any business carried on by him.

In the course or furtherance of any business

The supply does not have to be made in the normal course of the taxable person's business. For example, the sale by a solicitor of a desk which has been used in his business is chargeable to VAT at the standard rate.

Output tax

The VAT due from a taxable person on taxable supplies made by him which are chargeable to VAT.

Input tax

The VAT charged on taxable supplies to a taxable person in respect of goods or services used or to be used by him for the purpose of any business carried on or to be carried on by him.

Recovery of input tax

A taxable person is entitled to recover so much of his input tax as is attributable under the General Regulations, Part V to such supplies as are specified in VATA 1983, section 15(2). These include (i) taxable supplies and (ii) supplies outside the United Kingdom which would be taxable supplies if made in the United Kingdom. In the context of recovery of input tax the expression 'taxable supplies' should be taken to include (ii). Input tax is recoverable at the end of the VAT accounting period in which it was incurred, irrespective of the amount of output tax due in the same period. Where the output tax due exceeds the input tax recoverable, the input tax is deducted from the output tax and payment of the balance then has to be made to Customs & Excise. However, if in any one period the input tax incurred exceeds the output tax due, the taxable person is entitled to receive payment of the difference from Customs & Excise and does not carry forward a credit balance to set off against future output tax due.

Fully taxable person

A taxable person who is able to recover all his input tax (usually because his own supplies are all taxable supplies).

Attribution of input tax

Input tax is attributable by a taxable person to a taxable supply where it is incurred by him on goods or services used or to be used by him *exclusively* in making that taxable supply and is attributable by him to an exempt supply where it is incurred by him on goods or services used or to be used by him *exclusively* in making that exempt supply.

Non-attributable input tax

Input tax on goods or services supplied to a taxable person which are used or to be used by him in making both taxable supplies and exempt supplies.

Partly exempt person

A taxable person who is not able to recover all his input tax (generally because some of it is attributable to exempt supplies). Such a person:

(i) may recover the whole of his input tax attributable to his taxable supplies;

(ii) may not recover any of his input tax attributable to his exempt supplies;

(iii) may also recover a proportion of his non-attributable input tax. The proportion is calculated by dividing the value (excluding VAT) of his taxable supplies by the value (excluding VAT) of all supplies made by him in the VAT accounting period, excluding in each case those supplies specified in the General Regulations, regulation 30(3).

This method of calculation (known as the standard method) is illustrated in Example 1 in Appendix D. Customs & Excise are authorised to approve or direct the use of other methods of calculating the amount of input tax recoverable in any period by a partly exempt person.

Tax invoice An invoice containing the particulars listed in the General Regulations, regulation 13(1).

Tax point The time when a supply is treated as taking place.

III VAT on your fees

Introduction

A supply of legal services made in the United Kingdom is a taxable supply and, assuming you are a taxable person, you should charge VAT at the standard rate on your fees. A supply of legal services made outside the United Kingdom is outside the scope of VAT (ie you should not charge VAT on your fees). This raises the question as to where a supply of legal services is made. The answer might appear obvious, but there are rules which require you, in certain circumstances, to treat the supply of your services as having been made outside the United Kingdom.

If your client is resident abroad, it is likely—though not invariably the case—that the supply of your services will be outside the scope of VAT. In addition, a supply of legal services relating to land situated outside the United Kingdom is always outside the scope of VAT regardless of whether your client is resident in the United Kingdom or elsewhere.

This summarises the position with effect from 1 January 1993. The old rules zero-rating certain supplies of legal services no longer apply and, whilst it is the case that many of the supplies which under the old rules were zero-rated now fall outside the scope of VAT under the new rules, there is one important difference which we shall highlight when we come to consider the new rules in detail. In order to appreciate this difference, however, it is necessary to remind ourselves briefly of the old rules.

The old rules

The supply of legal services to your client would have been zero-rated if either:

(a) the services related to land situated outside the United Kingdom; or

(b) the services did not relate to land and either:

  (i) your client belonged outside the EC and the Isle of Man; or

  (ii) the services were supplied to your client in his business capacity (and not in his private capacity) and, in that business capacity, he belonged outside the United Kingdom, but within the EC.

This was because such services fell within VATA 1983, Schedule 5, Group 9 ('International Services').

The new rules

The services, the supply of which was previously zero-rated under the old rules, have been removed from VATA 1983, Schedule 5, Group 9 by The Value Added Tax (International Services and Transport) Order 1992. Were it not, therefore, for the changes to the rules for determining where a supply of legal services is made, the supply of such services would have become standard-rated.

A supply of legal services is not chargeable to VAT if it is made outside the United Kingdom (VATA 1983, section 2(1)). The Value Added Tax (Place of Supply) Order 1992 provides that with effect from 1 January 1993:

(a) A supply of services relating to land is to be treated as made where the land is situated (article 5).

(b) A supply of services falling within VATA 1983, Schedule 3 (reproduced in Appendix B) is to be treated as made where the recipient of those services 'belongs' if either:

(i) he belongs in a country other than the Isle of Man which is not a member of the EC; or

(ii) he is a taxable person who belongs in a country which is a member of the EC other than the country in which the supplier belongs (article 16).

VATA 1983, Schedule 3, paragraph 3 includes legal services other than those relating to land.

Accordingly, the supply of legal services to your client will fall outside the scope of VAT and you should not charge VAT on your fees if either:

(a) the services relate to land situated outside the United Kingdom; or

(b) the services do not relate to land and either:

(i) your client belongs outside the EC and the Isle of Man; or

(ii) your client is a taxable person who belongs outside the United Kingdom, but within the EC.

A list of EC members appears in Appendix A.

These new rules are illustrated by the flow diagram opposite. Examples of the application of the new rules appear as Examples 2, 3 and 4 in Appendix D.

In applying the new rules, therefore, three questions may have to be considered: do your services relate to land, where does your client belong and is your client a taxable person?

Do your services relate to land?

The Value Added Tax (Place of Supply) Order 1992, article 5 provides that a supply of services such as are supplied by 'estate agents, auctioneers, architects, surveyors, engineers and others involved in matters relating to land' are to be treated as made where the land in connection with which the supply is made is situated.

VAT on your fees

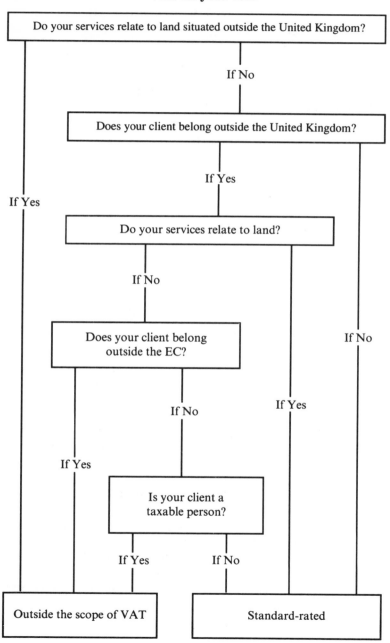

No further guidance is given in identifying when your services relate to land, but Customs & Excise Notice 741 stated in the context of the old rules that a supply of services where the land element was merely incidental should not be zero-rated. One of the examples given of where the land element is considered to be incidental was the legal administration of a deceased person's estate which may include property located outside the United Kingdom.

Where does your client belong?

In order to determine where your client, as the recipient of your services, belongs for VAT purposes, you should refer to VATA 1983, section 8 (3) and (4). This may be summarised as follows:

(1) If your client is an individual and the supply of your services is received by him otherwise than for the purposes of any business carried on by him, he is to be treated as belonging in whatever country he has his usual place of residence.

(2) In any other case, your client is to be treated as belonging in a country if:

(a) he has his business establishment or some other fixed establishment there and no such establishment elsewhere; or

(b) he has no such establishment (there or elsewhere) but his usual place of residence is there; or

(c) he has such establishments both in that country and elsewhere and the establishment of his at which, or for the purposes of which, your services are most directly used or to be used is in that country.

For these purposes:

(i) a person carrying on a business through a branch or agency in any country is treated as having a business establishment there; and

(ii) 'usual place of residence', in relation to a company, means the place where it is legally constituted.

This question was considered in *Binder Hamlyn v Customs and Excise Comrs* [1983] VATTR 171, which was concerned with the supply of services by a firm of chartered accountants to a company incorporated in Scotland. The company operated exclusively in Jamaica and had no 'establishment' in the United Kingdom other than the address of its registered office being at the accountants' office in Scotland. It was held by the Edinburgh VAT Tribunal that the registered office of the company was 'some other fixed establishment' within (2)(a) above and, therefore, by virtue of (2)(c), the company belonged in the United Kingdom on the basis that the services in question were more 'directly used' at the registered office. This decision was criticised in an article in *British Tax Review* 39 (1985) but has been followed in subsequent VAT tribunal decisions.

When is the relevant time for determining where your client belongs? The tax point is the time when a supply is treated as taking place but we understand that Customs & Excise look not at the tax point, but at when the services are actually performed. Customs & Excise's view, although not entirely consistent with the way in which VAT works, has a certain even-handedness about it.

Is your client a taxable person?

In the United Kingdom a taxable person is a person who is, or is required to be, registered for VAT (VATA 1983, section 2C(1)). Customs & Excise take the view that a taxable person for the purposes of article 16 means a registered taxable person (ie registered in the country where the services are received). This will simplify the application of the new rules: to have to establish whether your client is a registered taxable person in another EC country may be a burden in itself, but it would be almost impossible to determine whether your client, if not so registered, is required to be. This need to establish whether your client is a registered taxable person comes about as a result of the difference between the old and the new rules to which we drew attention earlier. Previously you only had to ask yourself whether your services were supplied to your client in his business capacity.

Immediately prior to publication of this book, Customs & Excise issued a Press Notice (19 March 1993) which offers a concession in cases where your client is unable to supply a VAT number. Customs & Excise maintain that a VAT number should always be requested, but alternative evidence of your client's 'business status' will be acceptable. This is not in accordance with the strict letter of The Value Added Tax (Place of Supply) Order 1992 and appears to be a retreat to the old régime where business status was the determining factor. Unless and until there is a change in the law, you should always seek your non-UK EC client's registration number, but if he is not registered, then, by concession, you will be able to rely upon alternative evidence of his business status in order to treat the supply of your services as outside the scope of VAT. Customs & Excise say that acceptable alternative evidence are certificates from relevant fiscal authorities, business letterheads or other commercial documents indicating the nature of your client's business status.

What enquiries do you have to make in order to determine whether your client is a taxable person?

Customs & Excise Press Notice dated 10 September 1985 states:

> 'As a general principle, the determination of liability to VAT is the responsibility of the taxpayer. In certain special cases the VAT liability of supplies of goods or services depends on the status of the customer receiving them. This can present problems for the supplier where the customer, innocently or otherwise, wrongly represents his status. Where this happens, the Commissioners of Customs & Excise will not hold the supplier responsible for failing to charge the correct amount of tax, provided they are satisfied that the supplier –
>
> (a) acted in good faith, and

(b) made normal and prudent checks and enquiries about the status of the customer and of any documentation of certification provided by him.'

In a statement in *The Law Society's Gazette* of 9 December 1992, The Law Society outlined the following practical steps which should be taken before treating supplies of legal services as outside the scope of VAT:

'(a) Obtain the VAT registration numbers of non-UK EC clients and include these on your invoice.

(b) Add the prefix "GB" to your VAT registration number.

(c) Change relevant invoices so that no VAT is shown for non-UK EC VAT registered clients (ie the "O" used for previously zero-rated supplies should be omitted).

(d) Omit outside-the-scope supplies from all VAT returns. These supplies are not required to be included in the statistical returns for foreign trade (EC sales lists) which relate to supplies of goods only, not services.

(e) When giving a VAT invoice to a non-VAT registered client elsewhere in the EC, ensure that UK VAT is shown at the standard rate.

(f) Remember to account for VAT on all supplies under (e) above.'

This statement is misleading in a number of respects:

- It in fact states that these are the steps that should be taken before 'zero-rating' supplies of legal services. The steps of course relate to supplies which are outside the scope of VAT.

- It would indeed be advisable to obtain the registration numbers of all your clients who are taxable persons outside the United Kingdom, but within the EC. When invoicing such a person, you should include not only his registration number, but the alphabetical code of the EC member state in which he is registered. These requirements are explained more fully in Chapter VI.

- The only step which one should take before treating a supply of legal services as outside the scope of VAT would be (a). Steps (b), (c) and (d) are procedures to be followed once you have satisfied yourself that the supply is outside the scope of VAT. Steps (e) and (f) do not belong in the list at all.

- Remember that if your client belongs outside the EC (and the Isle of Man), the supply of your services (other than those relating to land in the United Kingdom) will always be outside the scope of VAT. The need to change relevant invoices referred to in step (c) applies equally to these supplies.

It remains to be considered what steps (if any) you are required to take in order to check whether the VAT registration number given to you by your non-UK EC client is valid. Examples of what registration numbers abroad should look like are set out in Appendix A and it will normally be sufficient for you to satisfy yourself that the registration number you are given conforms with the appropriate example. If, however, you have suspicions about the validity of a registration number, Customs & Excise recommend that you should check with your local VAT office.

Transitional provision

Whilst the requirement to treat relevant supplies as outside the scope of VAT came into effect on 1 January 1993, the Customs & Excise Press Notice dated 5 January 1993 gives you until 1 July 1993 to obtain the VAT registration numbers of your EC clients abroad and permits you to apply the old rules (ie those relating to the zero-rating regime) in determining whether the supply of your services is outside the scope of VAT.

Input tax attributable to supplies outside the scope of VAT

As a taxable person, you are entitled to recover the input tax attributable to any supply of your services which is outside the scope of VAT just as if it were a taxable supply (VATA 1983, section 15(2)(b) and the General Regulations, regulation 32).

VAT and commission

If, in the course of acting for your client, you receive commission from a third party, you are obliged by the Solicitors' Practice Rules 1987, rule 10 to account to your client for that commission (subject to a *de minimis* limit which is currently £20).

If you set off the commission against the amount you charge your client, Customs & Excise at present allow you to charge VAT on the net amount of your fees, rather than the gross amount including the commission. This policy applies to all taxable persons who receive commission from a third party in connection with making a supply to a customer. However, *The Law Society's Gazette* of 9 September 1992 reports that Customs & Excise have claimed that solicitors should be treated as a special case because of the application of the Solicitors' Practice Rules 1987, rule 10. The report continues that following representations made by The Law Society, Customs & Excise have indicated on an informal basis that they accept that solicitors are not to be treated differently, but that all taxable persons will be required to charge VAT on the gross amount of their fees with any commission then being deducted to arrive at the net figure.

The authors consider this to be the correct treatment. The Law Society say that they are also minded to agree, but that doubts have been expressed by other professional bodies. Until agreement can be reached and revised guidance is published, Customs & Excise have advised that solicitors may continue to charge VAT on the net amount of their fees after setting off any commission.

IV VAT on disbursements

Introduction

A solicitor, in the course of his practice, is often required to pay for goods or services supplied by others. It is common for all such payments to be referred to as disbursements and to be treated as such when billed to a client. This indiscriminate treatment is wrong.

The correct VAT treatment of the different types of payment is not always immediately obvious, but it is important for a solicitor to identify the nature of each payment for the following reasons:

- in order to determine whether the payment should be made out of his office account or his client account;
- in order to ascertain how he should account to his client for the payment;
- in order to establish whether the payment, when billed to his client, should be subject to VAT and, if so, at which rate;
- in order to identify who, if anyone, is entitled to treat as his input tax any VAT included in the payment;
- in order to avoid committing an offence under the VAT legislation;
- in order to avoid committing a breach of the Solicitors' Accounts Rules.

Terminology

General expenses

Payments which form part of the expenses which you would normally incur in the course of providing services to your client may not be treated as disbursements for VAT purposes. These are referred to as **General Expenses**, and are treated for VAT purposes as forming part of your services. Included within this definition are all the general overhead expenses which you incur such as rent and electricity, but also payments in respect of items which might be more directly referable to the client in question, such as postage, telephone charges and courier fees. Even certain expenses which are quite clearly incurred on behalf of a particular client, such as hotel and travelling expenses, fall within this definition. Other payments which are to be treated as General Expenses are included within Appendix C.

It should be stressed that the identification of a payment as either a General Expense or a disbursement may require special care. It is not the description of the payment which determines its nature but the circumstances in which the supply was arranged. This is why, in regard to certain of the items listed in Appendix C, it has been necessary to say 'usually'.

Take, for example, search fees. Searches, whether at the Land Registry or the Companies Registration Office or elsewhere, are undertaken in the normal course of a solicitor's practice, but sometimes they are undertaken not merely as part of your overall service, but also to obtain for your client the benefit of a supply provided by a third party. The distinction may be highlighted by looking at the circumstances in which a solicitor makes a company search. If you do so solely for the purpose of providing yourself with information which will enable you to advise your client more fully, the search fee should be treated as a General Expense. If, on the other hand, you are instructed by your client specifically to make a company search and to present him with the results of the search, we would have little hesitation in saying that the search fee may be treated as a disbursement. This also applies to trade mark searches and patent searches.

In a normal conveyancing transaction, a solicitor will undertake a variety of searches including local searches and Land Registry searches. Rarely will these searches be undertaken on the specific instructions of your client, but they will normally result in the issue of a certificate which will be placed with your client's deeds and become his property. To this extent, you will be obtaining for your client the benefit of a supply provided by a third party and the search fee may be treated as a disbursement, rather than as a General Expense.

Photocopying, whether your firm does its own or engages an outside agency to do it on its behalf, will normally be undertaken in the course of providing legal services to your client and, in such cases, the relevant charges will fall to be treated as a General Expense when billed to your client. Similarly the photocopying charges of other firms when they supply you with photocopies of documents which you require in the course of providing legal services to your client amount to General Expenses. Where, however, your client asks you to supply him with photocopies of documents in your possession, the photocopying charges, when billed to your client, fall to be treated as a General Expense if you undertake the photocopying in-house and as a disbursement if you arrange for an outside agency to do this.

There has been continuing debate concerning the VAT treatment of telegraphic transfer fees (see, for example, *The Law Society's Gazette* of 21 February 1990 and 18 November 1992). Customs & Excise have made it clear that such fees are to be treated as General Expenses and this is consistent with the principles which are set out above.

Disbursements

The word 'disbursement' has a special meaning for VAT purposes. Customs & Excise use the term to mean a payment made by a solicitor as paying agent for his client in respect of goods or services supplied to that client.

The VAT Guide states that you may only treat a payment to a third party as a disbursement for VAT purposes if:

(a) you acted as the agent of your client when you paid the third party; and

(b) your client actually received and used the goods or services provided by the third party; and

(c) your client was responsible for paying the third party; and

(d) your client authorised you to make the payment on his behalf; and

(e) your client knew that the goods or services for which you paid would be provided by a third party; and

(f) your outlay is separately itemised when you invoice your client; and

(g) you recover only the exact amount which you paid to the third party; and

(h) the goods or services for which you paid are clearly additional to the supplies which you yourself make to your client.

Strictly applied, these criteria exclude many of the payments which tend to be regarded as disbursements. The main obstacle is criterion (c), that your client was responsible for paying the third party. This is essentially a question of fact, but if you analyse the payments which you make on behalf of your client you will discover that few qualify as disbursements in Customs & Excise's sense of the word.

The VAT Guide gives stamp duty as an example of a disbursement. When you pay stamp duty on behalf of your client, you are clearly acting as his agent, the responsibility for the payment falling squarely on him. Other clear examples of disbursements for VAT purposes include Companies Registration Office fees, court fees and Land Registry fees. In this context, payments such as estate agent's commission or another party's costs also spring to mind—they are your client's responsibility—and indeed these qualify to be treated as disbursements for VAT purposes.

Payments which amount to General Expenses do not qualify to be treated as disbursements mainly because criteria (c) and (h) will not have been satisfied: eg your client is not responsible for paying your telephone bill and the calls you make to him are incidental to and not additional to the supply of your legal services.

There is another type of disbursement which is made in respect of a supply which you have arranged on behalf of your client, additional to the supply of your own services (so it is not a General Expense) but does not qualify to be treated as a disbursement for VAT purposes because one or more of the criteria set out in the VAT Guide (normally criterion (c)) has not been satisfied. We refer to this type of disbursement as an **Agency Payment** in order to emphasise that it has been made in respect of a supply received by you as agent for your client. We restrict use of the term **Disbursement** to those payments which qualify to be treated as disbursements for VAT purposes.

We have already given some examples of Disbursements. Examples of Agency Payments include Counsel's fees, advertising expenses and the fees of foreign lawyers; others are included in Appendix C.

Method

General Expenses

- The original supplier's invoice (if any) will always have been addressed to you and not to your client.
- Any VAT charged on that original supply may be treated by you as your input tax.

- Some General Expenses are debited to the particular client in your accounts. Others are not. For example, you would probably debit your client with hotel expenses but you might not with telephone charges or postage.

- Whether or not debited to the particular client in your accounts, you may or may not choose to itemise them in your invoice to your client.

- If you choose to itemise a General Expense in your invoice to your client, you should show the VAT-exclusive amount as a head of your charges and not as a disbursement.

- A General Expense itemised in your invoice will attract VAT at the standard rate if your services are standard-rated and will attract no VAT if your services are outside the scope of VAT.

- The VAT treatment of a General Expense will follow that of your services and this is so regardless of whether the original supply to you was itself standard-rated, zero-rated, exempt or outside the scope of VAT. For example, if your services are standard-rated and you include postage as a separate item in your invoice, VAT must be charged at the standard rate on that item notwithstanding that VATA 1983, Schedule 6 provides that 'postal services' are an exempt supply. Conversely, if your services are outside the scope of VAT, so too are all General Expenses itemised in your invoice to your client, including those (eg courier fees) which attracted VAT at the standard rate when supplied to you.

- By special arrangement between the Law Society and Customs & Excise, where your client himself pays for your hotel accommodation and/or transport and these items are not itemised in your invoice, they will not be treated as part of the supply of your services. Accordingly, if the supply of your services is chargeable to VAT at the standard rate, your client should be asked to pay for the hotel and/or travelling expenses himself; this is particularly important where your client will be unable to recover the whole of the VAT chargeable.

Disbursements

This section deals with 'Disbursements', namely those payments which qualify to be treated as disbursements for VAT purposes. Agency Payments are dealt with later.

- Since one of Customs & Excise's criteria is that your client was responsible for paying the supplier, it will normally be the case that the supplier's invoice (if any) will have been addressed to your client.

- Whether the supplier's invoice is addressed to you or to your client, you are not entitled to treat any VAT charged on the supply as your input tax.

- If your client is a taxable person, he will be entitled to treat any VAT charged on the supply as his input tax and if the supplier's invoice is addressed to him, you should send it to him to enable him to do so.

- If the supplier's invoice is addressed to you, your client will be prevented from treating any VAT charged on the supply as his input tax. Therefore if your client is a taxable person and VAT is charged on the supply you should either return the invoice to the supplier and ask him to issue an amended invoice to your client or treat the payment in the same way as an Agency Payment (see below). The latter course will be simpler and just as effective in practice.

- A Disbursement may be paid either by you (whether out of your office account or your client account) or by your client direct. If the Disbursement is paid by you, you should seek reimbursement by your client either by including it in your invoice or in a statement of account or other request for payment in accordance with the Solicitors' Accounts Rules. If the Disbursement is paid by your client direct, it should not feature in your invoice or at all in your accounts.

- If the Disbursement is paid out of your office account and reimbursement by your client is to be sought by including it in an invoice, this may either be done immediately (because it exceeds the amount which you have agreed or are prepared to lay out on his behalf) or in due course when you next render an invoice. If immediate reimbursement is required, you should either render an interim invoice (see Example 5 in Appendix D) or a disbursements only invoice (see Example 6 in Appendix D).

- If you include a Disbursement in an invoice to your client you should show as a disbursement the total amount (including any VAT) paid to the supplier but you should not yourself charge VAT on this amount (see Example 7 in Appendix D).

- It is worth remembering that to include Disbursements in your invoice has the unnecessary effect of inflating the bottom line of your invoice.

Agency Payments

This section deals with payments which do not qualify to be treated as disbursements for VAT purposes but which are nevertheless commonly referred to as disbursements.

- It will normally be the case that the supplier's invoice (if any) will have been addressed to you.

- If, however, the supplier's invoice is addressed to your client, you may treat the payment in the same way as if it were a Disbursement (see above) even though it might not strictly qualify to be treated as a disbursement for VAT purposes.

- A special procedure exists for dealing with the payment of Counsel's fees (see Chapter V).

- Where no VAT is charged on the supply to you (because the supplier is not registered for VAT or because the supply is zero-rated, exempt or outside the scope of VAT) it makes no difference for VAT purposes whether you pay the supplier or your client pays the supplier direct. If you pay the supplier, you should seek reimbursement from your client either by including the amount paid to the supplier in your invoice or in a statement of account or other request for payment in accordance with the Solicitors' Accounts Rules. If included in an invoice to your client, you should show as a disbursement the amount paid to the supplier and you should not charge VAT on this amount (see Example 7 in Appendix D). Beware, however, of the reverse charge to VAT on supplies received from abroad (see Chapter V).

- Where VAT is chargeable on the supply and the supplier's invoice is addressed to you, the supply may be treated as having been made both to you and by you. This means that there are two separate supplies for VAT purposes. First, the supply to you in respect of which you are entitled to treat as your input tax the VAT charged by the original supplier. Secondly, when you invoice your client, the onward supply by you to your client on which you are required to charge VAT at the rate applicable to that supply and he may treat any VAT so charged as his input tax (assuming he is a taxable person and your services were used by him for the purpose of his business). The VAT treatment of the onward supply follows the VAT treatment of the supply of your services. In other words, if the supply of your services is standard-rated, you should show the amount (excluding VAT) as a disbursement in your invoice and charge VAT on the amount at the standard rate (see Example 7 in Appendix D). If, on the other hand, the supply of your services is outside the scope of VAT (see Chapter III), then you should show the amount excluding VAT as a disbursement in your invoice but *not* charge any VAT (see Examples 2 and 4 in Appendix D). The VAT charged on the supply to you will be recoverable in full as your input tax so you will not be left out of pocket.

- You will only be able to recover any VAT charged by the original supplier if his invoice is addressed to you and you pay him out of your office account. Even if there are sufficient funds in your client account, payment should be made out of your office account but you may use client account funds to reimburse your office account provided that in so doing you observe the Solicitors' Accounts Rules.

V Special cases: Counsel's fees and reverse charge on supplies received from abroad

Counsel's fees

The fee which you pay to Counsel is an Agency Payment. Assuming Counsel is registered for VAT, its VAT treatment depends upon whether the fee note is addressed to you or to your client (see Chapter IV).

The treatment is simpler where the fee note is addressed to your client and he pays Counsel himself. To this end, a special procedure has been agreed between Customs & Excise and the Bar Council whereby it is possible to treat the supply of Counsel's services as having been supplied directly to your client. This entails re-addressing Counsel's fee note by adding your client's name and address and the word 'per' before your own. You should then ask your client for a remittance in favour of Counsel and send this, together with the re-addressed fee note, to Counsel's clerk. Counsel's fee note will only become a tax invoice once receipted and this should be passed to your client thus enabling him to treat the VAT charged as his input tax (assuming he is a taxable person and the supply of Counsel's services was used by him for the purpose of his business).

Where your client is resident overseas and, following rules similar to those set out in Chapter III, the supply of Counsel's services falls outside the scope of VAT, you are entitled to certify Counsel's fee note accordingly, adding, in the case of a client who is a taxable person in an EC state other than the

United Kingdom, your client's VAT registration number there. Your client should be asked to pay the amount of Counsel's fees excluding VAT. This certification procedure only applies in cases where you choose to re-address Counsel's fee note and his services are thus treated as having been supplied directly to your client.

Where you choose not to re-address Counsel's fee note, then assuming Counsel is registered for VAT, you may treat the supply of his services as having been made both to you and by you. You will be entitled to treat as your input tax the VAT charged on Counsel's supply to you; this is so regardless of whether the onward supply by you is itself standard-rated or outside the scope of VAT. For this purpose, you should ask Counsel's clerk to send the receipted fee note to you.

You should show as a disbursement in your invoice the amount of Counsel's fees (excluding VAT) and, if the supply of your services is standard-rated, charge VAT at the standard rate on Counsel's VAT-exclusive fee. As explained in Chapter IV, if the supply of your services is outside the scope of VAT, Counsel's VAT-exclusive fee should be shown in your invoice as a disbursement but you should not charge VAT on it.

Having put in funds to pay Counsel, you should bear in mind the changes made by the Solicitors' Accounts Rules 1991. These provide that remittances received in respect of unpaid Counsel's fees (and other professional fees) must be paid into your client account.

Where your invoice covers your own fees as well as Counsel's (with or without other disbursements), any remittance received from your client must be split: the VAT-exclusive amount of Counsel's fees should be paid into your client account; the balance (comprising your fees, other disbursements and all VAT included in your invoice) may be paid into your office account. This can be done either by paying the whole amount into your client account and then transferring the balance into your office account within seven days, or the cheque itself can be split.

If you have delivered a disbursements only invoice to your client in respect of Counsel's fees, any remittance received from your client in settlement of your invoice must be paid into your client account.

When you pay Counsel you should ensure that payment is made from your office account to enable you to treat the VAT on Counsel's fees as your input tax. Only when Counsel has been paid may you transfer to your office account money held in your client account for payment of Counsel's fees.

In cases where Counsel is not registered for VAT, it makes no difference for VAT purposes whether you re-address Counsel's fee note or not. If you pay Counsel you should seek reimbursement from your client either by including Counsel's fees in your invoice or in a statement of account or other request for payment in accordance with the Solicitors' Accounts Rules. If included in an invoice to your client, you should show Counsel's fees as a disbursement and you should not charge VAT on this amount.

Reverse charge on supplies received from abroad

VATA 1983, section 7 provides that where 'relevant services' are supplied by a person who belongs outside the United Kingdom to a person who belongs in the United Kingdom and such services are received by him for the purpose of any business carried on by him, then the recipient of the services is treated as having made a taxable supply of the services to himself in the course of his business.

For this purpose, 'relevant services' means services of any of the descriptions specified in VATA 1983, Schedule 3, other than services which would have been exempt supplies if made in the United Kingdom. Schedule 3 is reproduced in Appendix B to this book.

This means that whenever you receive relevant services from abroad (eg you instruct a foreign lawyer or accountant):

- these services will be treated for VAT purposes as having been made by you to yourself;

- when you pay for the services, you should issue yourself with a tax invoice in respect of those services in an amount equal to the amount which you paid to the foreign supplier, but charging yourself VAT at the standard rate (see Example 8 in Appendix D);

- the tax point to be shown on your invoice is the date on which you send your payment to the foreign supplier;

- the VAT which you charge yourself must be accounted for as your output tax, but may be recovered as your input tax;

- if you are recovering the payment from your client, you should include in your invoice to him the amount paid to the foreign supplier (but not including the VAT which you charge yourself) and charge VAT on that amount at the standard rate if the supply of your services is standard-rated.

VI   Tax invoices

The rule used to be that a registered taxable person was only required to provide a tax invoice when making 'a taxable supply to a taxable person'. Now the General Regulations, regulation 12(1) reads as follows:

> 'Save as otherwise provided in these Regulations, or as the Commissioners may otherwise allow, where a registered taxable person –
>
> (a) makes a taxable supply in the United Kingdom to a taxable person,
>
> (b) makes a supply of goods or services other than an exempt supply to a person in another member state, or
>
> (c) receives a payment on account in respect of a supply he has made or intends to make from a person in another member state,
>
> he shall provide such persons as are mentioned above with a tax invoice.'

In other words, a tax invoice:

- must be provided where you make a supply of legal services in the United Kingdom to a taxable person;
- need not be provided where you make a supply of legal services in the United Kingdom to a person who is not a taxable person;

- must be provided where you make a supply of legal services to a person (whether a taxable person or not) outside the United Kingdom, but within the EC;

- must be provided where you receive a payment on account from a person (whether a taxable person or not) outside the United Kingdom, but within the EC in respect of a supply you have made or intend to make;

- need not be provided where you make a supply of legal services to any person outside the EC (and the Isle of Man).

You do not have to have three forms of invoice. Use of an invoice containing the combined requirements for invoices to be provided to taxable persons in the United Kingdom and to persons in other EC member states will ensure that the General Regulations are always complied with.

Although regulation 12(1) uses the word 'provide', the General Regulations themselves and VATA 1983 refer also to the 'issue' of a tax invoice. In trying to discover why this apparent distinction is made, we have considered whether one involves more or less than the other. In *Customs & Excise Comrs v Woolfold Motor Co Ltd* [1983] STC 715, it was contended that the use of 'provide' for certain purposes meant that 'issue' did not connote the provision to the client of a tax invoice. McNeill J rejected this contention and concluded that the issue of a tax invoice requires its provision to (ie delivery into the possession of) the client. Whether this means that 'provide' and 'issue' are synonymous or that 'issue' involves something more than 'provide' remains unclear. However, our reading of the General Regulations leads us to conclude that 'provision' is intended to mean something more than 'issue' and that the provision of a tax invoice entails (i) issuing it to the client and (ii) giving it or sending it to him. The point at which a tax invoice is 'issued' will vary from practice to practice but in most cases it will normally be when the invoice has been addressed to your client, dated and given an identifying number.

In order to comply with the General Regulations, regulation 13, your tax invoice must show:

(a) an identifying number;

(b) the time of supply;

(c) the date of issue of the invoice;

(d) your name and address;

(e) your VAT registration number (with the prefix 'GB' where your supply is made to a person, whether a taxable person or not, outside the United Kingdom but within the EC);

(f) the name and address of your client;

(g) where your supply is made to a taxable person outside the United Kingdom but within the EC, your client's registration number prefixed with the alphabetical code of the EC member state in which he is registered;

(h) the type of supply;

(i) a description sufficient to identify the particular goods or services supplied;

(j) for each such description:

   (i) the quantity of the goods or the extent of the services,

   (ii) the rate of VAT, and

   (iii) the amount payable, excluding VAT, expressed in sterling,

   (This requirement is only applicable to supplies made to a taxable person in the United Kingdom);

(k) the gross total amount payable, excluding VAT, expressed in sterling *(the requirement to express the amount in sterling is only applicable to supplies made to a taxable person in the United Kingdom)*;

(l) the rate of any cash discount offered;

(m) the total amount of VAT chargeable expressed in sterling.

A model form of invoice containing the combined requirements and identifying the constituents appears on pages 34 and 35 followed by a few words of explanation.

ROSENCRANTZ & GUILDENSTERN

Solicitors

1601 Denmark Hill, London SE5 8WS   **(d)**

Telephone: 071-201 2011

Arthur Rosencrantz
Bernard Guildenstern
Charles Voltimand
David Cornelius
Edward Osric

To: **(f)**
      (g)

Invoice No: **(a)**

(e)   VAT Regn. No: GB 999 1601 99

Our Ref:
Date: **(c)**

Tax Point: **(b)**

Period of supply	Charges	Disbursements	VAT	
			Rate %	Amount
(j)(i)	Supply of legal services **(h)**			
	(j)(iii)			

	£	£
Total Charges:	£	
Total Disbursements:	£	
Total excluding VAT:	£ (k)	
Total VAT:	£ (m)	
TOTAL DUE:	£	

(i)

The time of supply of your services – the tax point

Rules are contained in VATA 1983 and in the General Regulations for determining the time at which a supply of goods or services is treated as having taken place. This is called the tax point.

The basic tax point for a supply of services is the date on which the services are performed (VATA 1983, section 4(3)) and is normally taken as the date on which all the work except invoicing is completed.

This basic tax point can be overridden by the creation of what the VAT Guide describes as an actual tax point which arises if either:

(a) a tax invoice (eg an interim invoice) is issued or payment is received prior to the basic tax point (VATA 1983, section 5(1)): in this case, the tax point applicable to the amount so invoiced or received is the date on which the invoice is issued or on which payment is received, whichever is the earlier; or

(b) a tax invoice is issued up to 14 days (but see below) after the basic tax point (VATA 1983, section 5(2)): in this case, the tax point is the date of the invoice (unless an earlier actual tax point has been created under (a) above).

Customs & Excise have extended this 14-day period to three months for solicitors and so, unless you issue an interim invoice, the actual tax point for the supply of your services will be the date of your tax invoice provided that the work was completed no more than three months prior to that date. If more than three months have elapsed, the tax point will be the date on which the work (other than invoicing) was completed.

The name and address of your client

The supply of your services is made to your client and your tax invoice must be addressed to him even if a third party is paying your fees.

Your client's registration number

The client's registration number will be prefixed with the alphabetical code of the EC member state in which he is registered. The alphabetical codes are listed in Appendix A.

A description sufficient to identify the supply

There is no need, for VAT purposes, to include in your tax invoice a detailed description of the work you have carried out: the description need only be 'sufficient to identify the particular services supplied'.

If your client is to have the benefit of a detailed account of your services, but is reluctant to have the precise nature of those services disclosed in a document which must be made available for inspection by third parties, a two-part invoice may be utilised, one containing the minimum information required for it to constitute a tax invoice, the other, whether or not including that information, containing a full description of the work you have carried out. The latter should be clearly marked 'This is not a tax invoice' if there is any possibility that it could be mistaken for one.

The extent of the services

Given that there is no requirement for a tax invoice to contain an extensive description of the services and that the corresponding requirement in relation to a supply of goods is 'the quantity of the goods', we take the view that 'the extent of the services' can only mean the period during which they were supplied.

VII The payment of a solicitor's fees by someone other than his client

Who pays the VAT?

Where one party to a transaction agrees to pay the other party's legal costs, the question arises as to which party should pay the VAT on those costs.

The answer to this question depends upon the terms of the agreement which the parties have reached. So an agreement to pay the other party's 'costs including VAT' is just that—irrespective of the ability of the other party to recover some or all of the VAT.

Where no mention is made of VAT and the agreement is simply to pay the other party's 'costs', it is generally assumed that the liability is one of indemnity. This has been endorsed by the Law Society on a number of occasions—see, for example, *The Law Society's Gazette* of 28 October 1992. The liability of the paying party therefore extends to such of the VAT on the costs as is not recoverable by the other party as his input tax.

Where your fees are to be paid by someone other than your client and the liability is one of indemnity, you will first need to ascertain whether your client is registered for VAT and, if so, whether your services were used by him for the purpose of his business.

1. Where your client is not registered for VAT or your services were used by him other than for the purpose of

his business, the paying party should pay your fees together with all the VAT.

2. Where your client is registered for VAT and your services were used by him for the purpose of his business:

    (a) if your client is a *fully taxable person*, the paying party should pay your fees excluding VAT and your client should pay the VAT;

    (b) if your client is a *partly exempt person* and your services were used by him exclusively in making taxable supplies, the paying party should pay your fees excluding VAT and your client should pay the VAT;

    (c) if your client is a *partly exempt person* and your services were used by him exclusively in making exempt supplies, the paying party should pay your fees together with all the VAT;

    (d) if your client is a *partly exempt person* and your services were used by him in making both taxable supplies and exempt supplies, the paying party should pay your fees together with the proportion of the VAT which your client is unable to recover. Your client should pay the balance of the VAT. The appropriate proportion will not normally be ascertainable until after the end of the VAT accounting period in which the tax point occurs and this factor might lead the parties to come to some alternative arrangement unless the amount of VAT involved is substantial in which case a provisional apportionment followed by a later adjustment may be justified. Beware of arrangements which defer the payment of VAT since, whether or not you have received payment, you will be obliged to account for the VAT within one month of the end of your VAT accounting period in which the tax point occurs.

Who is entitled to recover the VAT?

The fact that someone other than your client may have agreed or been required to pay for your services does not affect the principle that if anyone is entitled to treat the VAT charged by you as his input tax, it is your client, the recipient of your services.

Provided that your services were used by him for the purpose of his business, your client will be able to recover:

    (a) all the VAT if he is a fully taxable person;

    (b) all the VAT if he is a partly exempt person and your services were used by him exclusively in making taxable supplies;

    (c) the appropriate proportion of VAT if he is a partly exempt person and your services were used by him in making both taxable supplies and exempt supplies.

None of the VAT will be recoverable by your client if:

    (a) he is not a taxable person;

    (b) he is a taxable person but your services were not used by him for the purpose of his business;

    (c) he is a partly exempt person and your services were used by him exclusively in making exempt supplies.

Under no circumstances is the paying party entitled to recover as his input tax the VAT charged by you on your fees and this is so even though he may have paid some or all of that VAT.

To whom should your tax invoice be provided?

In circumstances in which the General Regulations require you to provide a tax invoice (ie where your services are chargeable to VAT at the standard rate and your client is a taxable person), it must always be provided to your client and this includes addressing it to him. The provision of a tax invoice to anyone else will render you liable to the payment of a penalty (Finance Act 1985, section 17(1)) and might also constitute a criminal offence (VATA 1983, section 39(1)) if it assists the person to whom you give or send it to treat the VAT fraudulently as his input tax. If the paying party requires a receipt, it should not take the form of a tax invoice and if there is any possibility that it could be treated as one, it should be clearly marked 'This is not a tax invoice'.

Legal services in insurance claims

According to the Customs & Excise Press Notice dated 31 December 1984, a policy-holder who is registered for VAT may treat as his input tax the VAT which is charged on legal services in connection with insurance claims relating to his business. This will apply whether you are instructed by the policy-holder himself or by the insurer on the policy-holder's behalf and whether or not the proceedings are, in practice, controlled by the insurer. It will also apply where you are instructed by an insurer exercising his right of subrogation to pursue or defend a claim in the name of the policy-holder.

What is the position where the policy-holder is not registered for VAT or the insurance claim does not relate to his business? Under these circumstances, the policy-holder is not entitled to treat the VAT which is charged on your services as his input tax, but is the insurer?

VAT Leaflet 701/36/92 (1 February 1992) suggests not. It states that legal services in relation to an insurance claim are 'normally' supplied to the policy-holder, not the insurer and that an insurer cannot treat as his input tax the VAT on a supply to a policy-holder.

This statement is correct as far as it goes. If your services are supplied to the policy-holder, then it is undoubtedly the case that the insurer is not entitled to treat the VAT charged on those services as his input tax. If, however, you are instructed by the insurer, it is to him that your services are supplied and it is he who, under the normal rules, is entitled to treat the VAT charged on your services as his input tax. We regard the Press Notice as an exception to the normal rules. Customs & Excise permit a policy-holder who is registered for VAT to treat as his input tax the VAT charged on your services in connection with an insurance claim relating to his business. It follows that if the policy-holder is to treat the VAT on your services as his input tax, the insurer cannot also do so. If, however, the policy-holder may not rely upon the Press Notice because he is not registered for VAT or the claim does not relate to his business, there is no reason why, in cases where your services are supplied to the insurer, the insurer should not be able to treat the VAT on your services as his input tax.

Since an insurer carries on either a partly or a fully exempt business and is therefore unlikely to be able to recover more than a small proportion, if any, of the VAT charged on your services, does any of this matter in practice? Unfortunately, the answer to this question is yes. You are required to issue your tax invoice to the person to whom your services are supplied and the issue of a tax invoice to anyone else will render you liable to the payment of a penalty (Finance Act 1985, section 17(1)).

We consider that when you are instructed by the insurer, you should regard your services as supplied to him unless the policy-holder is registered for VAT and the claim relates to the policy-holder's business, in which case he may rely upon the Press Notice and you may treat the supply of your services as having been made to him. Only on this analysis do both the tax invoice and the input tax correctly end up in the hands of the same person.

In summary, therefore, we recommend that where you are instructed by an insurer in relation to an insurance claim:

    (a) if the policy-holder is registered for VAT, and is able to recover all the VAT on your fees and the claim relates to his business, you should (i) issue your tax invoice to him and ask him to pay the VAT on your fees, which

VAT he will be entitled to recover as his input tax, and (ii) send a copy of your invoice (marked 'This is not a tax invoice') to the insurer and ask him to pay your fees excluding VAT;

(b) in all other cases, you should issue your tax invoice to the insurer and ask him to pay your fees together with the VAT, which VAT he will be entitled to treat as his input tax.

You may not of course treat your services as supplied to the policy-holder if you are advising the insurer in the context of a dispute with the policy-holder. In such a case, your tax invoice should always be issued to the insurer.

Costs as part of the consideration

Customs & Excise Notice 742, paragraph 45 states that where a tenant agrees to pay some or all of the landlord's costs in connection with the grant of a lease, the payment will be treated by Customs & Excise as forming part of the consideration for the grant.

The landlord's legal and other costs represent consideration for the supply of services to the landlord and the VAT on those costs may not, as we have seen, be recovered by the tenant.

However, the costs also form part of the consideration for the grant of the lease. If the landlord has elected to waive the VAT exemption, the grant of the lease will be a taxable supply by the landlord to the tenant chargeable to VAT at the standard rate. The costs paid by the tenant should be included in a tax invoice to be issued by the landlord to the tenant and will be subject to VAT. It should be noted that the landlord will be required to charge the tenant VAT on the fees and all disbursements included in his tax invoice even if any of those disbursements were not subject to VAT when invoiced to the landlord.

Since the costs paid by the tenant are treated as part of the consideration for the grant of the lease, the tenant will be entitled to treat as his input tax the VAT charged by the landlord if the tenant is registered for VAT and has taken the lease for business purposes.

According to Customs & Excise Notice 742, this principle does not apply to the payment of landlord's costs by the tenant other than on the grant of a lease. In that Notice, Customs & Excise say that they do not regard payment by the tenant of the landlord's costs in respect of the exercise by the tenant of any right under the lease itself (eg to assign the lease) as consideration for any supply by the landlord to the tenant. However, Customs & Excise have announced a new policy effective from 1 December 1992 reported in *The Law Society's Gazette* of 28 October 1992. If, under the terms of the lease, the tenant exercises a right which requires the consent of the landlord but the landlord cannot unreasonably withhold consent to the exercise of the right, the payment by the tenant of the landlord's costs will not amount to consideration for any supply by the landlord. However, where the landlord has absolute discretion as to whether or not to grant consent to the exercise of the right, payment by the tenant of the landlord's costs is regarded as consideration for a separate supply by the landlord to the tenant on which VAT will be charged by the landlord to the tenant. The supply by the landlord will normally be the grant of consent such as consent to assign or underlet but the report in *The Law Society's Gazette* goes on to say that VAT will not be chargeable if 'the right sought to be exercised would constitute an exempt supply'.

The meaning of this exception is not clear. Since the supply by the landlord is the grant of consent, it is difficult to see how the right sought to be exercised has any bearing on the nature of the supply by the landlord. The only reasonable interpretation that we can put upon this exception is where, for instance, the tenant seeks to exercise a 'right' to take a new lease of the premises or, perhaps, a lease of additional premises. According to the new policy, where the landlord has complete discretion as to whether consent is to be granted for the exercise of the right (in which case it seems wrong to describe it as a 'right') payment of costs incurred by the landlord will be regarded as consideration for a separate supply. In such a case, the separate supply would not be the grant of consent as such but the grant of the new lease and, as stated above, if the payment by the tenant of the landlord's costs is regarded as part of the consideration for the grant of the lease, then the landlord will not charge VAT on the costs if the new lease itself is an exempt supply.

Where a tenant is required to pay the landlord's costs under the terms of the lease pursuant to an obligation to indemnify the landlord (eg costs in connection with the preparation of a schedule of dilapidations) such an obligation is an indemnity and the payment would not be regarded as consideration for any supply by the landlord to the tenant.

Customs & Excise Notice 742, paragraph 45 refers only to the payment by a tenant of the landlord's costs. In the authors' view, the principle applies more extensively, so that VAT will be chargeable by the vendor on the payment by a purchaser of the vendor's costs in connection with the sale of any property where the sale is chargeable to VAT at the standard rate. Indeed, there is no reason why the principle should not also extend to any form of transaction in which one party requires the other party to bear some or all of his costs.

Costs in connection with the transfer of a business as a going concern

The VAT (Special Provisions) Order 1992, article 5 provides that where the conditions set out in the Order are met, the transfer of a business as a going concern is to be treated as neither a supply of goods nor a supply of services. This means that VAT should not be charged on the transfer.

Strictly speaking, input tax incurred in connection with a transaction which amounts to the transfer of a business as a going concern is not recoverable because it does not relate to a taxable supply. However, we understand that the practice of local VAT offices varies. Sometimes the input tax is treated in the same way as input tax on the general overheads of the business, ie if the person is a fully taxable person, the whole of the input tax will be recoverable and if the person is partly exempt, then only the appropriate portion will be recoverable. Sometimes, however, Customs & Excise will allow the input tax to be recovered in full if the transaction (ignoring the rules relating to transfers of going concerns) would have been standard-rated, but allowing none of the input tax to be recovered if (again ignoring the rules) the transaction would have been exempt.

If you are advising a client in connection with the transfer of a business as a going concern and the other party to the transaction is to be responsible for the payment of your fees, your client will need to establish the extent to which the VAT on your fees may be treated as his input tax before you can ascertain the extent to which the paying party should pay the VAT on your fees.

Costs in connection with the acquisition or disposal of shares in a company

In their Press Notice dated 11 January 1993, Customs & Excise declared that costs incurred by a business in respect of certain activities are not incurred in the course of business and thus will not be recoverable as input tax. One such activity is the acquisition or disposal of shares and if one party to a transaction of this nature is responsible for payment of the other party's costs, the indemnity should extend to the VAT on those costs.

Paying for another party's costs

If your client has to pay another party's costs, neither he nor you will be entitled to treat the VAT charged as input tax. If you pay another party's costs on behalf of your client, whether out of your office or client account, it is better practice not to include this payment in your invoice, but should you do so, you should show as a disbursement the total amount including VAT and not yourself charge VAT on this amount.

VIII   Bad debts

Relief from VAT on bad debts in respect of supplies made on or after 1 April 1989 is available if all the following conditions are satisfied:

- you have already accounted for VAT on the supply and paid it to Customs & Excise;
- the supply was made for a monetary consideration;
- you have written off the debt in your accounts and transferred it to a separate bad debt account; and
- the debt is over six months old (ie six months after the tax point).

The relief only extends to the VAT on the part of the debt that remains unpaid. Equally the VAT element of any payment received after relief has been claimed must be repaid to Customs & Excise. If you are insured against your bad debts including VAT, your bad debt relief entitlement is not affected notwithstanding payment by your insurer.

For relief to be available in respect of supplies made before 1 April 1989, you have to show that:

- your client has become formally insolvent;
- you have already accounted for the VAT on the supply and paid it to Customs & Excise; and
- the supply was made for a monetary consideration.

What amounts to a formal insolvency is set out in Part II of VAT Leaflet 700/18/91 (1 April 1991).

Appendix A: EC membership, alphabetical codes and example registration numbers

Existing membership

Country	Alphabetical code	VAT equivalent	Number example
Belgium	BE	TVA* or BTW**	BE 123 456 789
Denmark	DK	MOMS	DK 12 34 56 78
France	FR	TVA	FR 12 123456789
Germany	DE	MWSt.	DE 12345678 9
Greece	EL	ΦπΑ	EL 12345678
Ireland	IE	VAT	IE 1234567A
Italy	IT	IVA	IT 12345678901
Luxembourg	LU	TVA	LU 123456 78
Netherlands	NL	BTW	NL 1234 56 789 B01
Portugal	PT	IVA	PT 123456789
Spain	ES	IVA	ES A12345678
United Kingdom	GB	VAT	GB 123 4567 89

* French
** Flemish

Countries which have applied for membership

Austria	applied: 1991, likely entry: 1995
Cyrpus	applied: 1990, likely entry: 2000
Finland	applied: 1991, likely entry: 1995
Malta	applied: 1990, likely entry: 2000
Norway	applied: 1992, likely entry: 1995
Sweden	applied: 1991, likely entry: 1995
Switzerland	applied: 1992, likely entry: 1995
Turkey	applied: 1986, likely entry: 2000+

Notes:
(1) The Isle of Man is treated as part of the United Kingdom for VAT purposes but is outside the EC.
(2) The Channel Islands are neither part of the United Kingdom nor within the EC.
(3) Monaco is part of the EC for VAT purposes (from 1 January 1993).

Appendix B: VATA 1983, Schedule 3

1. Transfers and assignments of copyright, patents, licences, trademarks and similar rights.

2. Advertising services.

3. Services of consultants, engineers, consultancy bureaux, lawyers, accountants and other similar services; data processing and provision of information (but excluding from this head any services relating to land).

4. Acceptance of any obligation to refrain from pursuing or exercising, in whole or part, any business activity or any such rights as are referred to in paragraph 1 above.

5. Banking, financial and insurance services (including re-insurance, but not including the provision of safe deposit facilities).

6. The supply of staff.

6A. The letting on hire of goods other than means of transport.

7. The services rendered by one person to another in procuring for the other any of the services mentioned in paragraphs 1 to 6A above.

8. Services –

   (a) of the transportation of goods which begins in one member State and ends in a different member State;

(b) of loading, unloading, handling and similar activities carried out in connection with services of the description specified in sub-paragraph (a) above;

(c) supplied by a person acting as agent for a disclosed, named principal consisting of the making of arrangements for, or of any other activity intended to facilitate, the making by or to his principal of a supply of a description specified in sub-paragraph (a) or (b) above;

which are treated as supplied in the United Kingdom by virtue of the recipient's having disclosed his registration number for the purpose of the tax chargeable in respect of the supply; and section 7(1) of this Act shall have effect in relation to the services described in sub-paragraphs (a) to (c) above as if the recipient belongs in the United Kingdom if, and only if, he is a taxable person.

Appendix C: types of payment

NOTE:
This appendix is produced for guidance purposes only. There is no substitute for analysing each type of payment by reference to the rules set out in Chapter IV.

AP = Agency Payment

GE = General Expense

DB = Disbursement

Advertising expenses	AP
Births, Marriages and Deaths – fees for searching Register of	usually GE (see Chapter IV)
Commons Registration search fees	AP
Companies Registration Office fees	DB
Company seal	AP

Company search fees	usually GE (see Chapter IV)
Company statutory books	AP
Completion monies	DB
Costs of another party	DB
Counsel's fees	AP (see Chapter V)
Courier's fees	GE
Court fees	DB
Designs Registry search fees	usually GE (see Chapter IV)
Designs Registry fees (other)	DB
Estate agents' commission	DB
Expert's fees	AP
Fax charges	GE
Foreign lawyer's fees	AP (but see Chapter V)

Hotel expenses	GE
Land Registry fees	DB
Landlord's registration fees	DB
Legal database search fees	GE
Local search fees	AP
Managing agents – fees for information	AP
Mortgage redemption monies	DB
Patent search fees	usually GE (see Chapter IV)
Patent Office fees (other)	DB
Patent agent's fees	AP
Photocopying charges	usually GE (see Chapter IV)
Postage	GE
Sheriff's fees	AP

Solicitors instructed to act as your agents – fees of	AP
Stamp Duty	DB
Sums paid in settlement of dispute	DB
Swearing fee paid to solicitor or notary: – where affidavit/stat dec is by you	GE
– where affidavit/stat dec is by a client or a third party	AP
Telegraphic transfer fees	GE
Telephone charges	GE
Telex charges	GE
Travelling expenses	GE
Trade mark search fees	usually GE (see Chapter IV)
Trade Marks Registry fees (other)	DB
Trade mark agent's fees	AP
Witnesses' expenses	DB
Wordprocessing charges	GE

Appendix D: examples

Example 1: Partial exemption calculation

(1) Input tax attributable to taxable supplies	=	£50,000
(2) Input tax attributable to exempt supplies	=	£12,000
(3) Non-attributable input tax	=	£28,000
(4) Value (excluding VAT) of all taxable supplies	=	£600,000
(5) Value of all exempt supplies	=	£200,000
(6) Value (excluding VAT) of capital goods sold	=	£40,000[1]
(7) Premium (exempt) received on assignment of lease	=	£50,000[2]

The proportion of non-attributable input tax recoverable (which is expressed as a percentage and rounded up to the next whole number) is:

$$\frac{(4) - (6)}{(4) + (5) - (6) - (7)} \quad \frac{£560,000}{£710,000} = 79\%$$

The recoverable non-attributable input tax is 79% of £28,000 (£22,120) so the total recoverable tax is £72,120, leaving £17,880 irrecoverable.

---

[1] To be excluded pursuant to the General Regulations, regulation 30(3)(a)
[2] To be excluded pursuant to the General Regulations, regulation 30(3)(b)(iii)

Example 2: Invoice to non-UK EC client registered for VAT abroad

You are instructed by Antonio Rialto, a Venetian merchant registered for IVA in Italy, in connection with his liability as surety for a debt owed to Shylock Limited. The following payments have been made:

Counsel's fees (AP)	£500.00 plus VAT of £87.50
Taxi fare to Heathrow (GE)	£20.00
Air fare to Venice (GE)	£300.00

and you wish to render an invoice.

ROSENCRANTZ & GUILDENSTERN
Solicitors

1601 Denmark Hill, London SE5 8WS
Telephone: 071-201 2011

Arthur Rosencrantz
Bernard Guildenstern
Charles Voltimand
David Cornelius
Edward Osric

To: Sig. Rialto Antonio, IVA Regn. No: IT 12345678901
        Via Portia 15b, Venice, Italy

Invoice No: (002)

VAT Regn. No: GB 999 1601 99

Our Ref: EO/VG
Date: 07.10.1993

Tax Point: 07.10.1993

Period of supply		Charges	Disbursements	VAT Rate %	VAT Amount
11 May-07 Oct 1993	Supply of legal services to date in relation to your proposed defence of the claim by Shylock Limited	1500.00			-

		£
Air fare	300.00	
		–
Disbursement		
Counsel's fees	500.00	–
		£ 500.00

Total Charges:	£ 1820.00
Total Disbursements:	£ 500.00
Total excluding VAT:	£ 2320.00
Total VAT:	£ 0.00
TOTAL DUE:	£ 2320.00

Example 3: Invoice to non-UK EC client not registered for VAT abroad

The facts are the same as for Example 2 except that Antonio Rialto is not registered for IVA in Italy.

With this in mind, when you flew to Venice to see him, you arranged for him actually to pay your air fare.

ROSENCRANTZ & GUILDENSTERN
Solicitors

1601 Denmark Hill, London SE5 8WS
Telephone: 071-201 2011

Arthur Rosencrantz
Bernard Guildenstern
Charles Voltimand
David Cornelius
Edward Osric

To: Sig. Rialto Antonio,
      Via Portia 15b, Venice, Italy

Invoice No: (003)

VAT Regn. No: GB 999 1601 99

Our Ref: EO/VG
Date: 07.10.1993

Tax Point: 07.10.1993

Period of supply		Charges	Disbursements	VAT Rate %	VAT Amount
11 May-07 Oct 1993	Supply of legal services to date in relation to your proposed defence of the claim by Shylock Limited	1500.00		17½	262.50

Disbursement		17½	87.50
Counsel's fees	500.00		
	£ 500.00		£ 353.50

Total Charges:	£ 1520.00
Total Disbursements:	£ 500.00
Total excluding VAT:	£ 2020.00
Total VAT:	£ 353.50
TOTAL DUE:	£ 2373.50

Example 4:   Invoice to USA client

You are instructed by Rosalind de Boys, who belongs in the USA, and who wishes to register her trade mark 'Ganymede' in the UK. The following payments are made:

Trade mark agents' fees (AP) £100.00 plus VAT of £17.50
Courier's fees (GE)   £40.00 plus VAT of £7.00
Trade mark application and
    registration fees (DB)   £185.00

Since Rosalind belongs outside the EC, you do not have to enquire whether she is registered for VAT (or any equivalent) in the USA in order to treat the supply of your services as outside the scope of VAT.

ROSENCRANTZ & GUILDENSTERN
Solicitors

1601 Denmark Hill, London SE5 8WS
Telephone: 071-201 2011

Arthur Rosencrantz
Bernard Guildenstern
Charles Voltimand
David Cornelius
Edward Osric

To: Mrs. R. de Boys,
      Orlando House, Optville, Idaho, USA

Invoice No: (004)

VAT Regn. No: GB 999 1601 99

Our Ref: DC/AJP
Date: 14.10.1992

Tax Point: 14.10.1992

Period of supply		Charges	Disbursements	VAT Rate %	VAT Amount
17 April 1992 - 14 Oct 1992	Supply of legal services to date in relation to the registration of the trade mark "Ganymede"	300 00			

		£
Courier's fees	40.00	
Disbursement		–
Trade mark agents' fees	100.00	–
Trade mark application and registration fees	185.00	–
		£ 285.00

Total Charges:	£ 340.00
Total Disbursements:	£ 285.00
Total excluding VAT:	£ 625.00
Total VAT:	£ 0.00
TOTAL DUE:	£ 625.00

Example 7:   Invoice showing the VAT treatment of General Expenses, Disbursements and Agency Payments

You are instructed by Miss Viola String in connection with the incorporation of a company to be called Cesario Limited and the taking of a lease in the name of that new company of premises at 1 Epiphany Road, Illyria, Surrey. The following payments are made:

Incorporation fee (DB)	£50.00
Fee on statutory declaration by you (GE)	£3.50
Local search fee (AP)	£60.00
Company search fee against landlord (GE)	£4.00 plus VAT of £0.70
Company seal (AP)	£20.00 plus VAT of £3.50
Stamp duty (DB)	£300.00

ROSENCRANTZ & GUILDENSTERN

Solicitors

Invoice No: (007)

1601 Denmark Hill, London SE5 8WS
Telephone: 071-201 2011

VAT Regn. No: GB 999 1601 99

Arthur Rosencrantz
Bernard Guildenstern
Charles Voltimand
David Cornelius
Edward Osric

Our Ref: BG/JP
Date: 25.05.1992

Tax Point: 25.05.1992

To: Cesario Limited,
       1 Epiphany Road, Illyria, Surrey

Period of supply	Charges	Disbursements	VAT Rate %	VAT Amount
1 Dec 1984 - 20 May 1992	Supply of legal services in relation to the incorporation of the company and the lease of 1 Epiphany Road	1800.00		17½	315.00

Company Search	4.00		17½	0.70
Disbursements				
Incorporation fee		50.00	-	87.50
Local search fee		60.00	-	
Company seal		20.00	17½	3.50
Stamp duty		300.00	-	
	Total Charges: £ 1807.50	£ 430.00		£ 319.81
	Total Disbursements: £ 430.00			
	Total excluding VAT: £ 2237.50			
	Total VAT: £ 319.81			
	TOTAL DUE: £ 2557.31			

Example 8: Reverse charge on supplies received from abroad

In the course of acting for your client, you receive advice from a lawyer abroad, who invoices you in sterling and charges £628.00.

ROSENCRANTZ & GUILDENSTERN			Invoice No: (008)
Solicitors			
1601 Denmark Hill, London SE5 8WS			VAT Regn. No: GB 999 1601 99
Telephone: 071-201 2011			
Arthur Rosencrantz			Our Ref: CV/JG
Bernard Guildenstern			Date: 13.02.1993
Charles Voltimand			
David Cornelius			Tax Point: 13.02.1993
Edward Osric			

To: Rosencrantz & Guildenstern
      1601 Denmark Hill, London SE5 8WS

Period of supply	Charges	Disbursements	VAT Rate %	VAT Amount
13 Feb 1993	Supply of legal services by way of reverse charge on the supply of services received from T.H. Macbeth & Co.,			

	£	
	£ 109.90	

Total Charges:	£	
Total Disbursements:	£	
Total excluding VAT:	£	
Total VAT:	£ 109.90	
TOTAL DUE:	£ 109.90	